Lily
Hope you have as much fu
reading this book as I did.

Hector and Daniela.

SUPER CHARGED

SUPER⚡
CHARGED

HOW OUTLAWS, HIPPIES,
AND SCIENTISTS
REINVENTED MARIJUANA

JIM RENDON

TIMBER PRESS
PORTLAND · LONDON

Copyright © 2012 by Jim Rendon. All rights reserved.
Published in 2012 by Timber Press, Inc.

The Haseltine Building
133 S.W. Second Avenue, Suite 450
Portland, Oregon 97204-3527
timberpress.com

2 The Quadrant
135 Salusbury Road
London NW6 6RJ
timberpress.co.uk

Printed in the United States of America
Text designed by Susan Applegate

Library of Congress Cataloging-in-Publication Data
Rendon, Jim.
   Super-charged: how outlaws, hippies, and scientists reinvented marijuana/Jim Rendon.—1st ed.
      p. cm.
   How outlaws, hippies, and scientists reinvented marijuana
   Includes bibliographical references and index.
   ISBN 978-1-60469-295-2
   1. Marijuana—History. 2. Marijuana—California—History. 3. Marijuana—United States—History. 4. Marijuana—Therapeutic use—United States—History. 5. Cannabis. I. Title. II. Title: How outlaws, hippies, and scientists reinvented marijuana.
   HV5822.M3R45 2012
   338.4'761578270973—dc23   2012013890

A catalog record for this book is also available from the British Library.

CONTENTS

ACKNOWLEDGMENTS

In states like California that have medical marijuana laws, an increasing openness about cannabis cultivation can make it easy to forget that the federal government still considers the plant to be a dangerous, illegal drug. Those who work with cannabis are always at some risk of arrest no matter how well they adhere to state law. Many, many people took a leap of faith by agreeing to speak with me for this book—people who opened their homes and gardens to me, spoke freely, and accepted me at their kitchen tables for more than a few excellent meals. Without their trust and their openness, I would have no book to write, no story to tell. I truly appreciate the trust that all of these sources have placed in me.

In particular I'd like to thank Jorge Cervantes. He opened many doors for me in a world where, for obvious reasons, doors do not always open easily. His kindness and interest in this project, his passion for the plant, and knowledge about the industry and those in it made much of this work possible. Mel Frank was a remarkable resource and I appreciate his willingness to field questions and clarify many of the more technical points on the plant and breeding. Kevin Jodrey and the staff at the Humboldt Patient Resource Center in Arcata have also been a fantastic source of information and they have been incredibly tolerant, letting me hang around and pester them with a barrage of questions.

I'd also like to thank Tim Ramos and Abner Kingman who read through far too many manuscript pages and offered up great insights that helped me draft the book as well as Emily Loftis for her help. I am indebted to my dear friends in southern Marin County who put me up, fed me, and tolerated my erratic schedule on my layovers on the way to points north. And, without the patience of my wife and two sons who dealt with my long absences while on research trips and my many late evenings writing, none of this would have been possible. Thank you.

INTRODUCTION

The *High Times* Medical Cannabis Cup in San Francisco is a kind of coming-out bash for medical marijuana, attracting thousands of enthusiastic smokers to a conference center on the edge of the city's South of Market neighborhood. It's one of a few annual gatherings put together by the magazine, which has been publishing articles about marijuana since the 1970s. This one, the second ever in San Francisco, is also a business event with companies selling products and entrepreneurs swapping business cards. Most remarkably, though, it is a broad-daylight, public, pot-smoking bonanza. The emphasis here is on the cannabis.

There is only one thing explicitly medical about this event: in order to enter the outdoor area beside the conference building where people are buying, selling, and smoking marijuana you need a recommendation from a physician. Conveniently, one is available on-site for $60.

Outside, in the smoking area, thousands of people are pressed together, moving from one booth to another in a kind of marijuana-infused version of a Middle Eastern bazaar. At booth after booth run by medical marijuana dispensaries, people are selling dozens of different types of walnut-shaped buds that are covered in resin glands containing delta-9-tetrahydrocannabinol, or THC, the compound that gets smokers high. And it's not just buds on display and for sale. Cannabis is available in an incredible variety of forms. There are tinctures made from extracts of the plant's active ingredients, and dozens of varieties of hashish or hash, a dense paste made up of those powerful resin glands. People are selling seeds and cuttings of the plant. Everywhere there are cannabis-laced foods—brownies, cupcakes, cookies, candy, chocolate. There is Funny Honey and even Chillo, a hemp-infused beverage complete with a marijuana-leaf logo.

Some of the dispensaries have brought mature marijuana plants with them. One plant, its branches weighed down by resin-coated buds that grow outward in long, thick bunches, bends out into the passing crowd. Every now and then someone will stop to smell the pungent buds. Other dispensaries have set up lounges with DJs playing hip-hop or electronic music. Some of the booths have vaporizers that blow hot air over the buds, heating them only to the temperature at which the resin vaporizes, leaving the plant matter unburned. One vendor has cut to the chase and is just handing out plastic bags filled with marijuana smoke to anyone who wants them. Another person is passing around a joint the size of a baseball bat. Everyone, everywhere, is smoking.

At the far corner of the space is a booth run by Harborside Health Center, the state's largest marijuana dispensary. Its founder, Steve DeAngelo, spoke on a panel earlier in the day highlighting some of the successes of the medical marijuana movement: a remarkable 15-year string of victories at the ballot box. Since California voters passed Proposition 215 in 1996, making it legal for people with a physician's recommendation to buy and grow marijuana, 15 other states and Washington, DC, have followed suit, allowing broad legal access to the plant for medical purposes. To many here, DeAngelo is a celebrity. He has been advocating and agitating to make marijuana legal since the 1970s. He's been a nightclub manager, concert promoter, and record producer. And, just six months after this event, he would star in "Weed Wars," a Discovery Channel miniseries about the state's marijuana business. In his trademark porkpie hat, his long dark brown braids hanging down on either side of his face, his tie and brightly colored shirt, DeAngelo looks a bit like a ringmaster, a kind of cannabis carnival barker. Watching as thousands of people squeeze past each other moving from booth to booth openly selling, buying, and smoking marijuana here—a scene that was once unimaginable—he can't help but smile. "This is really amazing, isn't it?" he asks.

As we talk, a man approaches and asks if he can get a picture of himself with DeAngelo. The man, short and stocky, is wearing a straw fedora. Stuffed into the hat are two long stems with buds on them, poking upwards like giant, green rabbit ears. He's got a small marijuana plant in one hand and a bong in the other. DeAngelo puts his arm around the man and smiles for the camera.

The carnival-like atmosphere surrounding cannabis in California is not restricted to these kinds of events. Dispensaries like DeAngelo's have proliferated across the state. Enthusiasts, those with serious medical conditions, and sometimes both can walk into any dispensary and choose from dozens of different kind of buds, hash, tinctures, or edibles. They can buy pipes, bowls, bongs, vaporizers, or pre-rolled joints. But all of these creative means of consumption and cannabis preparation are just the tiny visible tip of the cannabis world. Behind all of that is a far-flung network of growers and breeders, the people who have been developing new growing techniques and creating new strains of the plant for nearly four decades. And ever since cannabis took off as a counterculture drug in the 1960s and 1970s, California has been America's epicenter of cannabis cultivation. With 12 percent of the nation's population, it produces more than 40 percent of the country's marijuana (and by some estimates over 70 percent). It is far and away the country's largest marijuana-producing state with a crop estimated to be worth $14 billion a year in 2006. Without the growers and breeders plying their trade in the hills of Humboldt and Mendocino counties or in the basements, garages, and warehouses in Los Angeles, Oakland, and other cities, there would be no cannabis to buy on dispensary shelves, no billion-dollar medical market at all. Yet strangely enough, these people are often overlooked in any discussion of medical marijuana or legalization.

Aaron Morales is one of those growers. He lives outside of Eureka in California's Humboldt County at the end of a road just past the kind of cookie-cutter suburban homes that ring cul-de-sacs across the country. Behind a six-foot-tall wooden fence is Morales' own ranch house. Inside, his two toddler-age children play on the couch next to his wife. Morales, who is tan and slim with long dark dreadlocks pulled back in a ponytail, walks me through a sliding screen door and out into the backyard. The house is up on a rise hemmed in by tall pine trees. If not for the light rain and fog, the Pacific Ocean might be visible. We walk around to the side of the house and into his greenhouse. The boards under our feet wobble on the uneven ground—the work of gophers that have been digging in the dirt. Inside, pepper plants and basil overflow from their pots. Strawberries are nearly ready to be picked. Lettuce and snap peas grow behind the berries. Morales explains that his children are vegetarians so he tries to grow as many vegetables as he can. On the opposite side of the greenhouse, about a hundred marijuana plants have recently begun to sprout buds.

Growing snap peas alongside marijuana plants is not unusual for Morales. His parents and his grandparents grew marijuana for personal consumption in southern California and he grew up around the plant. He moved north to Eureka in 1996 for many of the same reasons that a lot of people move: he wanted his kids to grow up in the country, in a place where he agreed with the values of the community. And he moved for work, aware that he could learn even more about cultivating for a living in Humboldt. California's northwestern counties have long been centers of marijuana cultivation. The area is wild and rugged. Redwood trees grow hundreds of feet tall, their tops disappearing into the fog. Steep mountains that rise thousands of feet above sea level create a craggy landscape where just about anything can be obscured. Much of the area is ranchland and second-growth forest recovering from decades of logging. Given the size of the area—Humboldt and Mendocino combined are nearly the size of New Jersey—it's not hard to find a remote corner in which to be left alone to do as you please. Starting in the late 1960s, hippies moved here and set up communities as part of the back-to-the-land movement, bringing the plant with them. Others looking for secluded places to grow moved into off-the-grid homes on remote hilltops, creating their own communities, a world of their own making with an economy increasingly dependent on growing marijuana. Mendocino County, with a population of just 87,000, has more than 22 stores specializing in the products needed to grow marijuana. For anyone looking to learn the trade, there could not be a better place to move.

Morales points out a plant that his oldest daughter Brittney, a student at nearby Humboldt State University, recently gave him. "She told me that she and her friends smoked this and it was so good, she brought me the plant. She named it Razzamatazz," Morales tells me. While we look at his plants—he is growing several popular and high-powered strains, OG Kush, Cheese, and Purple Kush—Brittney drops by and lights up a joint. She is studying botany with an eye to bettering her understanding of the cannabis plant, though even at Humboldt State, no one can actually study the cannabis plant itself. Instead, she applies the knowledge learned in the classroom to what her father is doing in the backyard. She wants to learn as much as she can about botany so that she can one day begin to create better medicinal strains of the plant. And she often pushes her father to get the strains that he is growing tested by labs that have recently opened to provide growers and dispensaries with information about the levels of the various compounds such as THC that are in the plant's resin glands.

Morales started growing for the medical market in 2007. Though California voters passed Proposition 215 in 1996, it took years before the law was clarified through court cases and by the state legislature. It is still implemented differently in counties and cities up and down the state as local government has wide latitude in how it applies the law. Proposition 215 allows doctors to recommend that patients consume marijuana as treatment for a dozen different conditions (including a broad category of "other" ailments). Most patients join a dispensary and buy their marijuana there. Patients can also grow their own marijuana or grow and sell to the dispensaries they belong to. Physicians can recommend that patients grow as many as 99 plants at a time, though cities and counties can set caps much lower than that. Growers and patients can belong to any number of dispensaries—some growers sell to 50 or more different dispensaries. Others like Morales, who grows in his greenhouse here and outdoors on other plots, sell directly to patients and to dispensaries.

For Morales, growing, selling, and smoking marijuana, even breeding new types of plants, is all as normal as getting up and going to work in the morning. In fact, it *is* getting up and going to work. And here, in the heart of California's marijuana country, Morales is no outlier—lots and lots of people are growing.

Yet outdoor growers here face an uphill battle. Morales switched from growing indoors under artificial lights to growing outdoors in part because of the environmental impact of using so much electricity to grow indoors. And, now that growers here can plant cannabis in the full sun instead of hiding it under trees, outdoor plants are very productive, yielding pounds of dried buds instead of ounces. Despite the advantages of growing outdoors, he says it is very hard to sell that marijuana to dispensaries—they are just not interested. Dispensaries tend to favor those who grow the plant indoors in tightly controlled conditions designed to maximize the crop yield. Indoor growers can harvest multiple smaller crops year-round, feeding the dispensaries' demand for smaller quantities of a variety of different types of high-quality marijuana. Those who grow outdoors harvest all at once in the late fall and can have hundreds of pounds of marijuana on hand that they need to sell at one time. Prices have fallen due to an influx of growers and dispensaries that have little interest in attempting to market the outdoor marijuana, which lacks the pristine look that medical marijuana buyers have come to expect. As a result, many of these outdoor growers who pioneered marijuana cultivation in northern California, and in many cases their children who are now growers themselves, feel that they are being pushed out of the business. Their communities and their way of life are being threatened, they say, not by any law enforcement crackdown, but, in a bizarre turn of circumstance, by the increasing openness brought on by the medical legislation.

That openness is very new. The plant has been outlawed across the United States since 1937 and subject to aggressive eradication efforts by law enforcement since the early 1980s. For most of the last 40 years, growers, breeders, dealers, and smokers operated in hiding, keeping their activities secret and on a relatively small scale. The creative and entrepreneurial whirlwind on display at the *High Times* Medical Cannabis Cup, the incredible diversity of the plant, is a direct result of the decentralized underground culture that has nurtured the plant for decades—from off-the-grid growers to untold numbers who set up lights to grow plants in a basement or closet. Growing became simple and widespread yet remained small scale and decentralized—and that has proven to be beneficial to the plant.

Cannabis, by some estimates, has been bred into roughly 2000 different strains. That is a remarkable level of diversity for such a widely cultivated plant. In contrast, much of our modern agriculture has sacrificed diversity for uniformity and increased yield. According to one study, in 1903 seeds for 307 varieties of sweet corn were available in the United States. By 1983, seeds for only 12 varieties were available. Cannabis, which has developed entirely outside of the law, has been on the opposite track. Yet shelter from modern agriculture alone would not necessarily have led to such diversity. The plant's biology also played a key role.

Nearly all plants have male and female reproductive systems on the same plant. Cannabis plants are different. Like only about 5 percent of plants, individual cannabis plants are either male or female. The plants are not pollinated by insects or birds; instead the male plants release their pollen into the wind. The buds that smokers purchase are really clusters of tiny female flowers that grow in bunches at the end of the plant's branches to catch the pollen as it blows by. The resulting seed carries the genes of both parents in different combinations. Many different males can pollinate one female, sometimes from miles away. The plant's genetic material is constantly mixing, helping new strains to develop with varied characteristics that are better adapted to the local environment and, in the hands of breeders, better able to meet varying consumer demands.

The plant is easy to pollinate and therefore easy to breed. As a result, most serious growers also breed plants. And over the decades people growing the plant all across the globe—and particularly in California and Holland—have developed myriad new strains. The plant expresses an incredible range of characteristics. Some reach 18 feet tall. Others are short and squat. The flowers, or buds, can range from almost day-glow purple and green to red, brown, yellow, and orange. Its scents can range from skunky to sweet and almost spicy to citrusy or fruity. And the potency can vary enormously. THC, which causes smokers to get high, is just one of the 80 or so cannabinoids that are concentrated in resin glands, tiny translucent structures that grow over nearly the entire plant and are most concentrated on the flowers of the unpollinated female plant. Since those glands, or trichomes as they are often called, are in the greatest abundance on the buds, growers try to maximize the size and number of buds that each plant produces.

Since the 1970s underground breeders have been pushing the plant to produce larger quantities of increasingly potent buds. The strains developed over the last few decades are so flower-heavy that the stalks will break under the weight of the buds unless they are supported by stakes or nets. Today marijuana can have five times the THC of the marijuana sold in the early 1970s. But that wholesale manipulation of the plant has had a significant drawback. Plants that are high in THC, which in addition to its psychoactive properties has been shown to help with pain, nausea, and other symptoms, tend to be low in another cannabinoid called cannabidiol, or CBD. Researchers are establishing that CBD has important medicinal properties, particularly as a pain killer and anti-inflammatory. Now some breeders who spent their careers developing strains high in THC for the illegal market are trying to develop strains that are high in CBD instead. Morales, for example, has planted dozens of seeds from a Spanish strain called Cannatonic—one of the few high-CBD varieties available today. He's been trying to find individual plants that have the right mix of CBD and THC, that grow well outdoors, and have an appealing smell and taste. He plans to isolate the best ones to grow and breed.

The work of these breeders taking place in the northern California hills and in warehouses and homes up and down the state is mimicking the efforts of scientists at one pharmaceutical company that is developing government-approved drugs from extracts of the cannabis plant. Rather than taking the common pharmaceutical approach of developing drugs by isolating an active molecule and synthesizing it, GW Pharmaceuticals, a firm based in the United Kingdom, actually breeds and grows marijuana plants that have high levels of particular cannabinoids that it needs for research and for drug production. And so it needs a large and varied bank of seeds in order to develop these strains. Since the plant is illegal nearly everywhere, the company wound up licensing its seeds from some of the most respected collectors in Holland who pioneered cannabis cultivation and breeding. For all of its lab coats, hundreds of millions in funding, and government-sanctioned research programs, the company's breeders are, in at least one fundamental way, doing the same thing as the breeders on Humboldt's ridge tops: they are manipulating the plant to bring out new desirable traits.

Now, with so many states allowing medical dispensaries, with companies like GW pushing the plant for its own medical products and research, the decentralized, outlaw world of the cannabis breeder and grower is crossing paths with the world that it avoided so long, the world of business, agricultural, and pharmaceutical norms. As these cultures collide, some old-time growers and breeders are sure to be pushed out by entrepreneurial newcomers as the business, the culture, and the plant move towards a more regulated environment.

Cannabis, however, will be tied to its underground history and all of the uncertainty that come with it for a long time to come. Even today the most basic information about marijuana is simply unavailable. No one knows with certainty how much marijuana is grown in the United States, in California, or even in Humboldt County. Even with the openness and the entrepreneurial investment resulting from the medical laws, there is no better way to track the market today than at the height of the drug war. The best guesses are based on how many marijuana plants are seized by law enforcement officials every year. Many estimates assume that the government seizes about 10 percent of the marijuana crop each year, but even that number is somewhat arbitrary. It does not account for variations in law enforcement strategy, funding, or even luck in finding particularly large grows one year or few large ones another year. And experts differ on how much marijuana might be harvested from the average seized plant. Others try to estimate based on usage statistics and some use both. Other statistics that would seem easier to obtain are similarly elusive. No one knows how many medical marijuana patients there are in California, as patients do not register with any government agency, they simply get a recommendation from a physician. Nor does anyone know how many dispensaries there are. Similarly, there is no official counting of distinct strains of cannabis plants. There is no official definition of what a strain is versus, say, an interesting individual plant. No one polices what exactly OG Kush is or whether the Sour Diesel strain for sale in a dispensary is really Sour Diesel.

Just about the only thing that is clear is that more cannabis is being grown in the United States every year and more of what is grown in the United States is being grown in California. In 2003 the government seized 1.2 million plants in the state. In 2010, it seized 7.4 million plants there—70 percent of all the marijuana seized in the United States that year. By just about any metric, there is a remarkable rush to grow marijuana in California. In researching and writing this book, I have tried to use official figures and those that have consensus among experts, but when it comes to cannabis, even most experts admit that just about everything is a best guess.

Because of this new openness about the plant, some growers such as Morales were happy to talk with me for the book using their real names. Others, who have had a long history in the illegal trade or who continue to sell to the black market, have asked that I not use their real names. In some cases I have used only their first names, in others they have requested that I use new names and change details to protect their identity. Some of those I spoke to use pseudonyms and have done so for decades, gaining notoriety in the cannabis world under these assumed names. In these cases I have used these pen names and pseudonyms to identify these people. There are explanations throughout the text that indicate when a person is being referred to by anything other than their full, real name.

Given the remarkable size of the marijuana industry (the government estimates there are over 17 million regular marijuana smokers in the United States and over 100 million have tried it) and the promise the plant holds as a medicine, cannabis is a fascinating and important story. This book tells the story of the cannabis world in transition, the underground breeders and growers who have shaped the plant we know today and how they and companies like GW are likely to shape its future as the plant moves from the illegal fringe to the scientific and perhaps even cultural and commercial mainstream.

1 MEDICAL MARIJUANA EVERYWHERE

Jorge Cervantes lives in a single-story suburban home just outside of Sonoma, California. The town center, with its historic mission, almost 1950s small-town feel, and links to the region's well-established wine industry, is worlds away from the San Francisco Medical Cannabis Cup and its explosive championing of cannabis culture. Yet Cervantes (his pen name, not his real name) is a pivotal figure in that world. In the early 1980s he wrote one of the first indoor grow guides. His book, *Indoor Marijuana Horticulture*, has sold over 700,000 copies and is available in seven languages. In his home office he still has a copy of the first printing with its hand-drawn diagrams of the plant and grow rooms. Through it and many subsequent volumes, he's taught generations of growers how to cultivate marijuana, indoors and out, and how to breed and produce seeds.

Cervantes had been living in Spain for decades, part of an expat cannabis community in Europe that established itself there in the 1980s and 1990s as a way to escape law enforcement crackdowns in the United States. Thanks to a new openness about the plant in California driven by the state's medical marijuana law, Cervantes recently returned here. He has shoulder-length graying blond hair and a neatly trimmed beard. His tiny Chihuahua, Mona, follows him closely everywhere he goes.

Behind the house is a small fenced-in yard that abuts his neighbors' yards on two sides. He's recently torn up much of the patio to put in large growing beds. The soil is turned up in large mounds. In the raised beds behind and alongside the house Cervantes will soon plant cannabis. Throughout the growing season, he will shoot a series of videos about these plants, posting them on YouTube. He used to appear in disguise in his videos, wearing sunglasses and a beret with long dreadlocks. Now, he has jettisoned his disguise. He appears wearing a t-shirt with a picture of himself designed out of tiny images of the THC molecule. Using his own backyard garden as a teaching tool, he shows viewers how to design their gardens, use compost, address problems with mold, lack of oxygen in the soil, and other issues. He appears examining the progress of the buds on his Green Crack, Blue Dream, Headband, and OG Kush plants. The exotic, sometimes nonsensical names of cannabis strains often have nothing to do with their characteristics. Sometimes they relate to the strains from which they are derived; other times they are just names dreamed up by their creators. On the videos and in real life, Cervantes' calm lilting voice and matter-of-fact way with the plants makes him sound a bit like the Mister Rogers of marijuana. And even in this bucolic, suburban Mister Rogers' neighborhood, growing marijuana in your backyard is just not a very big deal.

A few months later I meet Cervantes at his friend's place in San Francisco's South of Market neighborhood, a former industrial area now filled with nightclubs, restaurants, and condominiums not far from where the San Francisco Medical Cannabis Cup was staged. Inside of an old brick industrial building, Cervantes' friend Marco (who has asked that I not use his real name) sets several jars filled with marijuana down on his large dining room table. He pops the lid off one, takes out a walnut-sized bud, and shows it to me. "This is Lamb's Bread," he says. "It's an heirloom strain." As he explains, Lamb's Bread is a strain of marijuana originally grown in Jamaica and, lore has it, was reggae legend Bob Marley's favorite. In today's market it's a relatively rare and valued strain. The bud Marco shows me, about the length of his thumb, is a pale green cluster of tiny cannabis flowers that smells citrusy and a little sharp. "It's an up, energetic high," he says. "No couch lock at all." He opens up another jar filled with a strain called Blue Cheese, takes out a bud and squeezes it between two fingers. "This one, when you touch it, it's perky almost, hard," he says. "We grow really good pot. I'll show you."

Marco leads me downstairs, through his garage to an unmarked door. As soon as the door opens we are met with the dense, musky smell of marijuana. We walk down a hallway, past marijuana plants on shelves in the hall and rooms to each side filled with plants to a space about the size of a small bedroom. Its cement floor, walls, and ceiling are all painted a pristine white. Lights inside reflective hoods hang from the ceiling, creating a glare so bright that, until my eyes adjust, I have to squint to see the waist-high tables on wheels that take up nearly every square inch of available space. Marco and I stand in the only place we can—a tiny gap between the tables and the wall.

Row upon row of marijuana plants, about 50 in total, sit atop the tables. The pale, bare stalks of the three-foot-tall plants have been trimmed of all excess leaves. Marco cuts the lower stems and leaves off to focus all of the plant's energy on producing the buds that grow above. The spindly, finger-like leaves jut out at eye level. In the tight space I have to crane my head back to see the small buds emerging from the stems in the plant's upper reaches. They are small, only a few inches long and covered in light hairs. "They're still early. These have a ways to go," says Marco reaching out to touch a thin branch of a nearby plant. "They smell great. Just kind of touch it and smell your fingers. It's real aromatic when it's raw. The smell's actually the best indication, at least for me, of how well the plant's doing."

All of the plants in this room are females. Females produce thousands of tiny flowers in clusters at the end of their branches, increasing the chances that a flower will catch pollen released by a male plant into the wind. Each seed carries the genes of both parents and each seed can carry different combinations of that DNA, allowing a range of characteristics to manifest in the offspring. The plant's psychoactive compound, THC, is concentrated in resinous glands, tiny translucent structures that are most concentrated on the female flowers. Since once a plant is pollinated, it begins producing seeds and stops producing resin, growers remove all males from their flowering rooms to enable them to grow seedless buds called sinsemilla that produce as much THC as possible.

Marco is a tinkerer and a software programmer and his knowledge and passion for problem solving and clean, elegant solutions is apparent everywhere in his urban, indoor marijuana farm. Indoor growers like Marco are able to control every aspect of the plant's lifecycle by manipulating its environment to meet the plant's needs and to push it for optimum production. He has programmed small computers (usually used in saw mills and other industrial facilities) to adjust the temperature, light cycle, and humidity in each of his many grow rooms here. Marijuana plants have essentially two stages of growth: the vegetative stage in which the plant simply grows, getting taller, broader, beefier, increasing its leaves, and the flowering stage when the plant puts its energy into producing flowers. When the days are long in the summer—14 to 16 hours or so—the plant is in its vegetative stage. When the days get short in the fall—down to about 12 hours or so—most cannabis plants begin to flower.

Marco keeps the temperature in these rooms in the 70s when the lights are on and in the 60s when the lights turn off. Humidity, always an issue in indoor grow environments because plants absorb water through their roots and expel water vapor through their leaves, is kept remarkably low thanks to dehumidifiers. Even watering is automated. While we stand in the room admiring his crop, a nozzle rises inside one of the large trays that hold the plants. Water flows from the nozzle—it's a bit like a low-pressure version of the lawn sprinklers used in public parks—filling the tray with a mix of water and liquid nutrients. Once the tray is filled, it's left to rest for 30 minutes while the plants soak up the water through their roots that trail out the bottom of the pots like tentacles from jellyfish. The water then flows back out through pipes that empty into the building's waste system. No human contact required.

The computer also controls the level of carbon dioxide in the facility. Plants absorb carbon dioxide and expel oxygen. Indoor grows, particularly one like Marco's where the air is not expelled (to keep the pungent and easily identifiable smell of marijuana outside his building to a minimum), have problems with a buildup of oxygen. Overall growth, and ultimately flower production, can fall off in environments that are too oxygen rich. Ambient air has about 400 parts per million of carbon dioxide.

Cannabis plants, Marco says, grow best with 1400 parts per million, so he adds it. When the level of carbon dioxide in the grow rooms starts to fall below that, the system turns on a tankless hot water heater mounted on the wall in the hallway. It burns propane to warm the water that runs through the heater. As it combusts, the clean-burning fuel produces primarily carbon dioxide, which is circulated through the grow rooms by fans (Marco monitors carbon monoxide levels in the rooms for safety).

We squeeze out of the room and walk back down the hall. Marco stops to point out a shelf full of two-foot-tall plants off to one side in the hallway. "This is the moms' room," he tells me. These are mother plants—individuals that are kept growing but not allowed to produce buds, sometimes for years. Growers cut branches off these plants and set them in a medium—soil or floral foam—so they sprout roots. After about 10 days the cuttings are ready to be planted. Though these are simply cuttings and this is a common type of propagation used in legal commercial agriculture, marijuana growers refer to these newly rooted cuttings as clones, since they are genetic copies of the mother plant.

Marco shows me a Lamb's Bread mother plant. It's a lighter green than some of the mother plants of other strains surrounding it. Its leaves are long and thin. Many of the plants that he showed me that were in flower were cut from this plant just two months earlier. The mother is not as tall as those that are flowering because it is constantly cut back to create new clones, but its stalk is wider, almost woody at the base because of its age. Growers have come to prefer working from clones. Cannabis plants grown from seed are often quite different from one another. Growing from a clone—a genetic copy of the mother—is one way that growers ensure they will grow and harvest the kind of marijuana they expect.

Every plant that Marco grows has a sticker on its pot that indicates the plant's history including which specific plant was the mother, the dates that it was transplanted, and when it went into bud. It gets a serial number that follows the plant from the day it is cut from the mother to the time the buds are harvested, dried, and trimmed of excess leaves. All of that information is tracked on a spreadsheet. That way Marco can easily assess which mother plants are producing the best cuttings and which may have problems. "You have to be crazy organized about this," Marco says. "Otherwise you just don't know what you are doing." Eventually, Marco plans to create an iPad app to track the data.

Retrofitting the building to create this grow house was expensive and incredibly complicated. "I had diagrams of the building, the air circulation, the ducting, where the trays go, the water, how the plumbing is put together—it's six or seven layers of diagrams that all add up to a room," he tells me. Like most growers, Marco had to get creative in how he chose to combine existing technologies like the flood trays and lighting systems, and how to implement new ideas like the water heater and even his automation programs. Every grower has his own approach. As Marco likes to say, ask three growers and you'll get four opinions. That is part of the creativity that keeps this pursuit interesting and evolving. He learned some of what he does from talking to other growers about their innovations and others will learn from his innovations. "Doing it right like this is a lot of work," he says. "But if you are going to do it, you have to do it right."

Marco is developing a reputation as a top-level grower. He routinely sells the Lamb's Bread strain to local medical marijuana dispensaries for $3600 a pound. That is a remarkably high price in a market that is increasingly flooded with marijuana, much of which sells to dispensaries for under $2000 a pound. Marco has invested a lot of money in this operation and expects it to pay.

Growing marijuana was not Marco's first choice of career path. He has smoked since he was a teenager and has grown for himself occasionally since college, but he has had other options. He has an MBA. He co-founded a Silicon Valley software company that was financed by one of the valley's top venture capital firms. Then, he says, he needed a change. "I wanted to try something entirely different," he says. Since he has had such a long-standing interest in and passion for tinkering with the plant and the technologies involved in growing as well as simply smoking, this was a natural choice. "I thought, 'why not try doing something you love,'" he says.

Marco sees important parallels between the entrepreneurial medical marijuana market and the culture in Silicon Valley that he recently abandoned. Given the tensions between the state (which allows medical growing) and the federal government (which views all cultivation as illegal) there are no large businesses involved in cultivation. "This is like the Silicon Valley model. There are lots of new start ups," Marco says. "There are a lot of people with different ideas who just think if this works it will stick and if not it won't. There is no R and D department, no approval for funding."

The fact that Marco and I are even having this conversation is remarkable. Once, the idea of someone with an MBA and a successful business deciding to grow marijuana would have been unheard of. But now, California's medical marijuana law has created a tolerance for small-scale growing in some cities and counties. People from across the country have been lured here to grow. In this competitive environment, an MBA can actually be quite useful. And that is not only the case in California. Medical marijuana laws have passed in 15 other states and Washington, DC, as of 2011. Most states with medical marijuana laws have a system of dispensaries or cooperatives where patients can become members and purchase marijuana. In some states members also grow the marijuana that is sold at the dispensaries. Colorado and California have the most open laws and the most established industries in the country. In Colorado, dispensaries are for-profit businesses unlike in most states where they must be non-profits. California created a medical exemption for what was already a massive illegal business. California has long been the nation's largest cannabis producer. Creating a medical exemption for growing, selling, and possessing marijuana over time allowed this industry to begin coming out from behind the shadows and to flourish in a way that it could not when it was illegal. Medical growers in Humboldt, Mendocino, San Francisco, and other places have, for the most part, been left alone to cultivate their crops. The law left regulation of dispensaries largely up to local communities. Some have overseen an explosion in the number of dispensaries; Los Angeles has over 500. In other parts of the state, there are no dispensaries at all.

California's underground cannabis economy is brought to life at Harborside Health Center, the state's largest medical dispensary. It is a temple to a new kind of upscale cannabis consumerism. The building is in an office park and, from the outside, could easily be mistaken for a dentist's or accountant's office. But here two security guards check to make sure those entering have valid medical marijuana cards. Inside, customers stand on the sisal carpet in a brightly lit room with white walls, high ceilings, and large windows—a kind of inviting, relaxing, almost bland environment. Customers wait behind rope lines like those at airport security, biding their time before they can step up to one of the 10 salespeople who work behind a long, blonde, wood counter. Once there, they can see 35 different strains of marijuana meticulously displayed. Here cannabis is handled and displayed with the kind of fetishized care reserved for expensive jewelry or custom-made suits.

Inside wood-framed, glass display cases, buds from dozens of strains of marijuana are displayed in petri dishes. Some of the buds have a reddish, or purple hue; others are yellow, or orange-tinged. A small card next to each dish displays the name of the strain: Kahuna, Jack's Haze, Red Congolese, Durban OG, and dozens of other cryptic names as well as the strain's THC content. Some strains contain over 20 percent THC—five times the potency of much of the marijuana available in the 1960s. The cards also list the percentage of cannabidiol or CBD, one of the compounds that studies show has significant effects on nausea, anxiety, convulsion, inflammation, and other symptoms and also may temper the effects of THC.

For decades anyone who wanted to smoke marijuana had to buy it from a black market dealer. Sometimes these connections had high-quality marijuana and sometimes they didn't. If your dealer didn't have the particular kind of marijuana that you were looking for, then you were out of luck. Today those with a doctor's recommendation can walk into any one of hundreds of dispensaries like Harborside and in one glance see more strains of cannabis than most pot smokers who bought from an illegal dealer would see in a lifetime. The culmination of decades of outlaw ingenuity and perseverance, the bounty and diversity of cannabis production is laid out before patients in every dispensary.

Harborside carries 35 of the estimated 2000 different strains of marijuana, an incredible range of diversity for any species. That diversity is a result of its unique history, one utterly different from just about any other plant grown in the developed world's industrial agricultural system.

Legal crops have had a tremendous infrastructure built up around them to help guide breeding and cultivation. Here in the United States, government research programs, universities, and private corporations all contribute to developing higher-yielding, pest-resistant strains of various crops that are well suited to long-haul shipping and express marketable uniformity. Universities and government agencies teach cultivation techniques and help develop new technologies, and the government subsidizes large swaths of the industry. This has resulted in a large-scale, high-yield agriculture dependent on chemicals that has been steadily whittling down the genetic diversity of our food supply. A 1983 study by the Rural Advancement Foundation (an old study but one of the few to look at such old records) found that between 1903 and 1983, 93 percent of the seed varieties sold by commercial seed banks in the United States were no longer available. Legal agriculture has spent the last hundred years chipping away at the genetic diversity of the plants that we cultivate. In 1903 seeds were sold for 497 varieties of lettuce. By 1983 seeds for just 36 varieties were available. Cabbage varieties fell from 544 to 28; radish varieties fell from 463 to 27. The genetic diversity in our food crops was decimated by the very mechanisms we set up to guide us to higher productivity, greater food security, and increased prosperity. Instead of diversity, we embraced scale and commoditization—the ability to truck a tomato across the country took precedence over the actual taste of the tomato and in the process we lost diverse local flavors, vast genetic resources, and small-scale, localized production.

Cannabis, on the other hand, has been outlawed in this country since 1937. The government has jailed growers, breeders, and those developing new cultivation technologies for cannabis. There are no bank loans to marijuana growers or investment capital for research or strain development or growing techniques. There are no legal protections for strains and no regulation of the finished product. All there have ever been are growers, breeders, seed companies, and dealers—outlaws willing to take a chance on the plant to earn money. All the traditional roles of breeder, researcher, agricultural advisor, farmer, educator, and even banker have not been eliminated in this underground market. They have simply been taken up by those passionate about the plant and willing to risk arrest. And because of the risk of arrest and the high price of the crop, even those with the largest grow operations are mere hobbyists compared to modern farmers of traditional crops, some of whom plant many hundreds of acres of a single crop at one time.

Because of the risk inherent in cultivating, many growers have remained isolated, talking only to those they do business with, and therefore information about new growing or breeding techniques, even seed stock, can travel slowly. As a result of this underground history, cannabis has a level of diversity almost unheard of in the legal agricultural world. There is general agreement that there are three subspecies of cannabis—sativa, indica, and ruderalis. Sativas are grown for hemp and both it and the indica subspecies are grown for medical and recreational use. Ruderalis grows wild in Russia, has little THC, and is not common in the United States. Much of the marijuana smuggled into the United States in the 1960s and 1970s were sativas from Mexico, Colombia, and Jamaica, and the marijuana usually included a lot of seeds. In the 1970s hippies brought back indica seeds from Afghanistan and

Pakistan. These plants are what breeders call landraces. Much like heirloom tomatoes, these landrace cannabis plants are native to a particular area and have not been subject to the intensive hybridizing so common on the recreational market. Growers in northern California began crossing these indica and sativa landrace plants with each other to improve yield, shorten the growing season, and to push for better or different types of highs. Breeders in Amsterdam in the 1980s and 1990s continued the work, creating indica and sativa hybrids that were shorter and broader—perfected for indoor growing—and that had even more THC.

Today, thanks to the quasi-legal medical market, companies selling seeds and cuttings of plants are opening up in California and Colorado and in many places in Europe too. These breeders are developing more hybrids with THC levels nearing 30 percent. Breeders have developed feminized seeds that will produce primarily female plants and what are known as auto-flowering plants, those crossed with ruderalis strains that always flower after a certain number of days regardless of the length of the day. In California and other states with medical laws, growers are producing huge numbers of clones as Marco does, some for their own cultivation and some for dispensaries to sell to their members.

Marco, like most dedicated growers, also breeds plants. In the hallway where he keeps his mother plants, he shows me one of his more exotic strains. He reaches up to the top of a rack of shelves filled with plants and takes down a short plant with long, light-green leaves—a strain called Tenerife, named for the island off the coast of Africa, from which it originates. "I've never seen this grown, I've only smoked it in Spain," he tells me. The plant is rarely found anywhere but on the island and has a long history there, making it one of the coveted landrace strains. In order to get the seeds, he had to spend time getting to know local growers there. "This is going to be real good breeding stock," he says.

Marco has a collection of seeds from over 50 different strains. He plans to grow each of them to see whether or not any of them hold promise for breeding. The cannabis connoisseur market that is driven by dispensaries like Harborside has created demand for new and more creative hybrids—marijuana that gives smokers different kinds of highs and buds with appealing scents and tastes. With so much breeding and so many new seed companies springing up in states that now have medical laws, grow-guide author Cervantes says the number of strains has been rising dramatically. Though no one has a definitive count, he estimates that there were about 1200 strains of marijuana in 2006, a number that ballooned to about 2000 in 2011. Others in the industry estimate that the number may be closer to 1000. No one really knows for sure as there have never been any centralized records or even definitions of what is and isn't a strain. Most, however, agree that the trend has only been upwards.

That rapid expansion of genetic diversity has not occurred without problems. Until very recently, few breeders in the United States ever kept records since a paper trail would create evidence that would bolster a criminal case. Communication was limited to trusted associates so advances in growing and breeding techniques, even the distribution of strains, often moved slowly, if at all. Entire genetic lines were lost in police raids. Because the plant was illegal, few ever conducted breeding with enough plants to realize its full genetic potential and many wound up inbreeding the plant in their effort to quickly stabilize strains to sell. Many of the analytical tools commonly used in breeding and crop development—gas chromatography to learn more about the chemical make up of new strains, peeking into the plant's chromosomes to learn when a strain is stabilized or what characteristics might lurk beneath the surface—were rarely applied to cannabis until recently. Labs that were willing to test the illegal substance simply did not exist. Though breeders over decades have all been taking their own personal approaches to their work, they have, for the most part, been pushing for similar characteristics: more powerful highs and better yields. And with breeding, whenever you select for something, you inevitably select against other traits. Certainly that's been the case with marijuana. Researchers are now finding out that CBD has important medicinal values. But the compound has been largely bred out of recreational strains in the search for ever more THC. Some breeders are now scrambling to track down rare CBD-rich strains.

Given the growing interest in and market for the medical uses of cannabis, it is no longer just those from the cannabis underground who are starting to study and use the plant. The UK-based firm GW Pharmaceuticals has developed a cannabis extract that has been approved to treat involuntary muscle contraction and tightness in patients with multiple sclerosis in Canada, the United Kingdom, New Zealand, and in several countries across Europe, as well as cancer pain in Canada. It is completing trials in the United States for approval by the Food and Drug Administration. The product is also in drug trials for approval to treat pain in cancer patients. Pharmaceuticals are usually created by isolating a particular active molecule and then synthesizing it. In contrast, the drug GW has developed, Sativex, is made from a cannabis extract. GW literally grinds up the leaves and buds of cannabis plants and, through an extraction and refinement process, creates a liquid extract that the patient sprays under the tongue. This spray is primarily composed of THC and CBD in a one-to-one ratio as well as trace amounts of other cannabinoids and terpenes, which act together to provide the therapeutic effect. According to the company's testing, Sativex does not get users high, likely because the CBD tamps down the high brought on by THC without interfering with its medicinal value. In order to make the spray, GW must grow an incredible amount of marijuana.

The company grows its marijuana in a complex of buildings in southern England. It has a special license from the government to grow in a country where the plant remains illegal and there are no medical exemptions as there are in California. From the minute I enter the building, the heavy odor of marijuana is unmistakable. Inside a room that is larger than a basketball court with a glass ceiling 20 feet high, the company grows 3000 marijuana plants at a time. Overhead, lights are strung up to augment the natural sunlight. All around me, row after row of marijuana plants, some as much as six feet tall, grow in deep-green clusters so dense that I can't see past the first row of plants.

The head horticulturalist, David Potter, shows me around. To say that he is enthusiastic about his job is a bit of an understatement. Potter loves the plant, the idea of breeding, creating new strains with medical value. The ability to legally grow this outlawed plant on this scale is thrilling for him. Potter even received a doctorate degree from Kings College, London, for studying the cannabis plant's medicinal properties. But Potter is no pothead. "I've never smoked cannabis," he tells me with a laugh. In fact, Potter learned how to grow marijuana on the job. "The first time I actually saw a cannabis plant coming to flower was in our very own glasshouse," says Potter. "Everyday was an adventure. Everything was so new. I must admit I was pinching myself at first."

GW licensed its vast seed stock from two of the biggest names in Holland's cannabis industry, Rob Clarke and Dave Watson. Clarke is one of the foremost experts on breeding and wrote *Marijuana Botany: Propagation and Breeding of Distinctive Cannabis*; Watson pioneered growing and breeding in Holland in the 1980s; and both have spent decades scouring the globe for rare landrace seeds. They were creating a collection for their own pharmaceutical company, HortaPharm, based in Holland, but were unable to secure the necessary funding to conduct research and create drugs from the plant. They likely had one of the largest libraries of cannabis seeds anywhere and they licensed it to GW.

Through extensive selection and breeding efforts, GW was able to develop two strains of cannabis that are used in Sativex, one that is very high in THC, another that is very high in CBD. It takes about 10 plants to make a year's supply of Sativex for one patient. Once the plant is harvested and dried, the leaves and buds are ground up, heated, and the cannabinoids are extracted from the plant matter and refined into a dark brown liquid. The company is continuing to conduct research on about 12 of the 80 known cannabinoids. Because the company develops medicine from extracts, each time it wants to study a new cannabinoid, it must develop a strain of the plant that is high in that particular compound.

In the hallway outside of the grow room, Potter shows me a plant with a large magnifying lens in front of it. The plant looks as if it has been dusted with powdered sugar—the white trichomes, which are as dense as frost on the buds, emanate outward and trail off as they get further away from the flower along the edges of the leaves. About 80 different cannabinoids and over 100 different terpenes, which give the plant its vast range of scents and flavors, from sweet to spicy to skunky, are contained in the trichomes. Under magnification, the trichomes look a bit like Seattle's Space

Needle—translucent orbs elevated on posts. "There is a little membrane, the skin if you will, keeping all of those terpenes and cannabinoids fresh," Potter says over my shoulder as I look at the magnified structures.

It's unclear what effect these terpenes might have on smokers, but smell and taste are the primary way that growers, breeders, and smokers identify particular strains of marijuana. And, it actually turns out to be accurate. Salvatore Cassano, an agronomist who has been studying marijuana in Italy for over a decade and consults on medical cannabis production, says his research shows that the levels of various terpenes correspond directly to the particular characteristics in the plant. The terpenes are the best way to differentiate between one strain and another. The cannabinoid and terpene molecules take three times as much energy to produce as its equivalent weight in sugars—much of the energy gained from photosynthesis goes to producing these trichomes. One hypothesis for why, Potter says, is that early in its history the plant grew in areas with poor soil but ample sunlight, like Afghanistan. If an animal bit off a portion of the plant, it would have a hard time growing again in an area like this because of the lack of nitrogen in the soil. But what the plant did have was lots of sunlight. So, it evolved to use that sunlight to create an abundance of cannabinoids and terpenes which can act as repellents to herbivores. The most important parts of the plant to defend are the reproductive organs in the flowers, which explains why the buds have the highest concentration of trichomes.

The psychoactive THC found in the trichomes mimics a compound that the human brain produces naturally. Our bodies already have receptors (called CB receptors) designed to bind to it. The THC activates receptors that can modulate activity in other neurotransmitters, affecting the brain and other functions in the body. That is what produces various "high" sensations and the medical benefits of the plant. The fact that the cannabis plant produces a compound that our brains are already hardwired to use is uncanny and, according to an article co-authored by John McPartland, an osteopath affiliated with GW who has done extensive research on cannabis, it's no coincidence. McPartland has written that these receptors, which are found not only in humans but throughout nature in other mammals such as monkeys as well as birds, fish, sea urchins, and even leeches, originally evolved in organisms 600 million years ago. That long predates the cannabis plant itself, which is about 34 million years old. He speculates that CB receptors and cannabinoids may have had ancestors in common dating back much further—before plants and animals diverged. These CB receptors may simply be a leftover from that time, one that our bodies activate naturally and we stimulate by smoking marijuana.

It is the complex combination of cannabinoids and terpenes that Dr. Geoffrey Guy, founder of GW Pharmaceuticals, wanted to utilize. He felt that there were benefits to be gained from creating a plant extract comprised of all these cannabinoids and terpenes rather than a drug based on a single molecule. "We knew that the whole plant was therapeutically effective," says Dr. Guy. "We didn't want to throw the baby out with the bath water."

GW is not a fly-by-night operation dabbling in cannabis production. The company is publicly traded, has marketing and distribution deals with Bayer, Novartis, and other large pharmaceutical companies. It has spent over $300 million on research to date. According to Lala Gregorek, a pharmaceutical industry analyst at Edison Investment Research, GW is in a good position to be a market leader in medicinal cannabis going forward. The company has expertise at navigating the complex and often daunting regulatory environment in Europe and the United States where there are serious barriers to any company that wants to seek approval for a cannabis-derived drug, let alone one that is an extract of the plant itself. "They are the only ones taking this extract approach and they have unique access to an extensive library of plant genetics," she says.

The company is professionalizing cannabis breeding, cultivation, and medical delivery in a way that is simply not possible in the United States even under the recently instituted state medical marijuana laws. Little dedicated scientific research on the medicinal benefits of cannabis goes on in this country. A 2009 American Medical Association report found that fewer than 20 randomized controlled trials involving fewer than 300 people have been conducted in the United States over the past 35 years on the medicinal value of smoked cannabis. That's in part because medical researchers hoping to study the effects of cannabis in the United States need to apply to the National Institute on Drug Abuse to obtain marijuana from its contract grower at the University of Mississippi. And the agency has a multi-layered, rigorous process, one that has often turned down those hoping to conduct medical research in favor of those researching the negative effects of the drug.

GW makes sure to distance itself from the medical marijuana movement, even chastising some organizations for citing their studies as evidence of the efficacy of cannabis. Because Sativex is a refined extract that has a particular and consistent makeup of cannabinoids and terpenes and it has been subject to the rigorous studies required for it to be approved as a medicine, Sativex, Dr. Guy says, is nothing like smoked cannabis. The company's studies should not be extrapolated to smoked cannabis. At the same time, some advocates fear that if GW's cannabis extracts are suddenly available for sale at the local pharmacy, then the argument for medical cannabis laws will fall flat. Who needs a medical exemption to buy marijuana when your doctor can prescribe you an FDA-approved extract? Yet GW is inextricably tied to cannabis' underground history. Without Clarke and Watson, pioneering growers and breeders, GW would not be where it is today.

Cannabis has been so shaped by its underground history that even legalization is unlikely to completely re-route the plant's trajectory. The small-scale growers that pioneered cultivation and breeding, the high-tech indoor growers like Marco, even the pharmaceutical companies, are inextricably tied to the plant's underground history—the diversity it gained and the price it paid for that genetic advantage. Regardless of how the cannabis business moves forward, it will only be shaped by that past. Many of the outdoor growers who pioneered marijuana cultivation and breeding could easily be pushed out as it lurches forward, displaced by indoor growers or large-scale greenhouse operations. Or, perhaps legalization in some states will take hold and all of these groups will find a place in an industry where the lines between outlaw and law abiding, recreational and medicinal, even right and wrong have all begun to blur.

2 HIPPIES START GROWING MARIJUANA

Far up in the steep, grassy mountains of California's northern coast, miles from the nearest paved road, Sean leads me down a dusty footpath through a grove of trees to a small shack. (Sean and his family have asked that I not use their real names or identify where they live since they have been, and continue to be, involved in the illegal marijuana trade. Their names and some details have been changed to protect their identities.) The one-room building, no bigger than most bedrooms, is equipped with a swamp cooler, a heater, a humidifier, a dehumidifier, several fans, and a temperature gauge. This far out, where the only source for electricity is a generator or solar panels, these are unusual luxuries. But they are completely necessary for drying marijuana. This is the cure room where Sean dries his crop.

Racks of wire shelves stand on either side of the cure room's door. What Sean refers to as his humidor is directly opposite the door. It's really just a freestanding, six-foot-tall rack of shelves with plastic pulled around it. Some of the shelves have plastic lining the bottom to restrict airflow. Others are open to let air circulate. The plastic wrapping the humidor's outside is held in place with large clips to restrict the flow of fresh air. All of the equipment in this room allows Sean to maintain constant temperature and humidity levels to dry his crop, regardless of the weather outside.

Over the years, he has developed his own intricate system for curing marijuana that involves moving it in and out of the humidor, drying it on shelves, beneath fans and at times away from fans, as well as in bags, all to slowly let the moisture out of the bud without drying it out too quickly or completely. "This is home-made; we kind of just figured it out," he says, while closing the clips on the humidor. "I'm sure no one else has this, but they definitely have something else they use."

Sean, who is 43 years old, has been involved with marijuana since he was a teenager, figuring out solutions as he goes. In 1976, when Sean was eight years old, his parents left San Diego and the outside world for this neighborhood in the rural mountains of northern California. They were inspired by the *Whole Earth Catalog*, a publication that provided a sort of counterculture road map for living off the land. It included everything from how-to articles for fixing Volkswagen engines and building geodesic domes to lengthy treatises by Buckminster Fuller, articles by environmental activist and early proponent of sustainable agriculture Wendell Berry, Timothy Leary, and even those attributed to The Black Panther Party. They wanted to get out of San Diego, raise their young son in the country and to try their hand at living closer to the land, something that sounded appealing, and even compelling in the pages of the *Whole Earth Catalog*.

"It was just such a wonderful time," says Sean's father, Paul, of the first few years when they had a sense of freedom and optimism about their new life and its possibilities. But after a few years, reality began to set in. The huts, tents, lean-tos, and other temporary buildings that people erected began to draw attention from the local government. Many locals were members of conservative logging and ranching families who had been here for generations and they were unhappy about the urban hippies taking over their secluded towns. Here, as in many similar communities across the country, the local government forced back-to-the-landers to comply with zoning and building codes, heaping expenses on people who were not financially prepared to build homes.

Paul used salvaged lumber and materials from their property, which had already been extensively logged before they bought it, to build their house. They erected a small, two-story log and plaster building with an open living room and loft-style bedrooms. The house is one of a couple hundred in a neighborhood that began as part of the back-to-the-land movement in the early 1970s and one where many people over the decades have grown marijuana.

But it did not start that way. Initially, few people grew marijuana here. There was little motivation to grow it in the 1960s and early 1970s. Smuggling it in from Mexico, Colombia, and Jamaica was fairly easy and since the plant sold for so little, there was hardly any reason to get into growing. People at the time usually smoked leaf, which is low in THC. If they managed to obtain a bud, it had gone to seed and had to be broken up and picked through to remove the seeds, which have no THC at all and give off harsh smoke when burned. When Paul first moved here in 1976, he had no intention of growing marijuana; then, only one person grew it here and that was mostly for personal consumption. Paul first tried growing in 1979 when he stuck a few plants in the ground behind his house.

It didn't take long before he became interested in growing on a larger scale. More people he knew were starting to grow and they were beginning to earn money from their crop. Paul says that the decision to grow cannabis wasn't much of a decision at all. Others he knew were developing the know-how for growing and the connections required to sell the marijuana. "Why would you refuse to do it when it's all right here in front of you?" Paul asks.

While we talk, Sean sits at a large table next to his homemade humidor. Underneath the table is a 25-gallon, blue Rubbermaid bin. Sean pulls the lid from the bin to reveal about a dozen football-sized bags of marijuana. These have just come back from the person he hires to trim his buds. Once marijuana is harvested, it must be dried on the various shelves and racks here and then trimmed. Trimmers remove the big leaves and stems from the buds and clip away all the leafy matter until all that is left is the resin-coated bulbous marijuana buds. Sean stacks the bags full of marijuana up on the table. Each bag has a square card in it that identifies the individual plant these buds were taken from, the strain—Romberry is on purple paper, Platinum Kush on yellow—the original rough weight, the trimmed weight, and which trimmer did the work. Sean records this information on a yellow legal pad that will later be burned. Paul and Sean, like other growers in this neighborhood, have learned through decades of experience not to keep any records related to marijuana growing—very little is ever recorded and that which is will be burned as soon as possible. He takes a very different approach, rooted in a long-standing fear of arrest, than someone like Marco who keeps detailed records on every plant.

Each of these dozen bags weighs somewhere between a half-pound and a pound-and-a-half. About a dozen pounds of marijuana are stacked up on the table in front of us. Sean is weighing the bags to verify the trimmer's numbers since trimmers are paid for their work by the pound (typically trimmers earn about $200 a pound). It's odd that Sean is just getting trimmed buds back in the summer. Since he is an outdoor grower, all of this marijuana was harvested last fall. But, he explains, since prices are down, he does not have enough money to get his marijuana trimmed all at once. He has to bag it and bury it, sometimes for six months or a year, and get it trimmed a little at a time when he has enough money saved up to pay his trimmers. Later Sean will sort and combine the bags of marijuana from a single strain to create uniform one-pound bags with even distributions of small and large buds.

As Sean weighs the bags and records the information, he tells me that over the years, as more people started growing here, cannabis cultivation became a bigger part of their culture, an important part of what set them apart from the rest of the world. "They were making their own space to do their own thing. They were making up a new world," he says of his parents and their friends in those first few years. "There was a strong sense of 'us and them' that was definitely communicated to me as a child. There were a lot of places that difference could be found and pot culture was just one of those places," he says. An important part of that culture was the annual harvest ball that would take place once the marijuana crop was in and cured and ready to smoke. "We had a harvest ball with big bouquets of pot and smoke coming down from the ceiling," he says. Remembering the scene from decades ago, he tells me that the air grew thick with marijuana smoke as his parents and their friends would play music and he would play with his own friends.

Sean's connection to the cannabis plant is just the most recent in a history that goes back thousands of years. The imprints of hemp fibers were found on shards of pottery in a 10,000-year-old settlement in Taiwan. Cannabis is generally believed to have originated in central Asia and spread by people from there to Europe, the Middle East, and around the globe. Over the millennia, people have used the plant for its fibrous stalk to make clothes, paper, and rope. Oil pressed from its seeds is used in cosmetics, industrial products like paints and lubricants, and as a food. And for thousands of years it has been used as a medicine and as an intoxicant. The ancient Greek historian Herodotus wrote about a funeral ritual of the Scythians, a nomadic, horseback riding tribe from central Asia, in 450 BC. To mourn the dead, the Scythians dug a pit, put in heated stones and covered the entire pit with mats—much like a Native American sweat lodge. They then climbed into the pit and put cannabis on the stones where it began to smoke. As Herodotus reported, "transported by the fumes, they shouted in their joy." Archeologists have found Scythian clothing made of hemp fibers. Some experts think that the Scythians and other similar nomadic groups may have been responsible for spreading the plant across parts of Asia and Europe.

Today cannabis is grown around much of the globe and is found in an incredible range of climates from the jungles of Vietnam, Thailand, and the Congo to the arid mountains of Afghanistan and Pakistan to extreme northern latitudes in Siberia. Although the nomenclature on *Cannabis* is in dispute, *Cannabis sativa* is widely accepted as a species, and *Cannabis indica* and *Cannabis ruderalis* are variously described as subspecies or even separate species. For the purpose of this book we will use the nomenclature that is common among the growers, breeders, and authors profiled. They treat *Cannabis sativa* as a species and *indica*, *sativa*, and *ruderalis* as subspecies of *Cannabis sativa*.

These three different subspecies of the plant have evolved, each adapted to somewhat different environments. Sativas are often found in warm climates such as Colombia, Mexico, Thailand, Jamaica, and Africa; they are also used for hemp production in the cooler climates of Europe, Canada, and elsewhere. The sativa subspecies can grow over 18 feet high. Some of its strains are high in THC and are known for an energetic and clear high. Others can be bred with almost no intoxicating THC and are used to make cloth, rope, and paper because of their long and tough fibers. The indica subspecies comes from India, Pakistan, and Afghanistan. Indica plants tend to be shorter than sativas and squat with broad, deep green leaves. Indicas are known for their very powerful, almost narcotic high. Ruderalis, the third subspecies, is found primarily in Russia. It's a small, hardy plant with virtually no THC. Ruderalis has a very different flowering mechanism than the other two subspecies. It flowers after a certain number of days regardless of the length of the day.

Cannabis was used as a medicine in the United States throughout the 19th century, but the widespread availability of aspirin by 1900 or so severely curtailed the market for cannabis tinctures here and elsewhere. It was used as a recreational drug as well. Cannabis became associated with blues and jazz musicians in the first half of the 20th century. As the drug grew in prevalence, state governments started outlawing it. The federal government outlawed it along with industrial hemp in 1937 and has done its best to eradicate it for the three quarters of a century since.

Cannabis gained notoriety in this country in part because the beats—poet Allen Ginsberg, authors Jack Kerouac and William S. Burroughs, their friend Neal Cassady, and others of that generation—found cannabis already in common use in the jazz scene in the 1940s and began smoking. They helped to popularize the drug and it became an important part of their own intellectual liberation from mainstream society. Burroughs, who gained a reputation for consuming any and all drugs with the zeal and insatiability of a child at an all-you-can-eat ice cream buffet, introduced Kerouac and the other beats to a range of drugs. When it came to marijuana, he became an important supplier. Martin Booth, in his book *Cannabis, a History*, writes that when Burroughs left New York City to stay on his East Texas farm between 1946 and 1948 he grew marijuana, which he then shipped back to his friends in New York. Booth also writes that Cassady, who worked for the railroad in the 1950s, smuggled large quantities of marijuana back from Mexico on trains. He argues that Cassady, who would go on to drive Ken Kesey and his Merry Pranksters cross-country on their LSD-fueled bus trip in 1964, was the first person to introduce significant quantities of Mexican marijuana to California and set the stage for the counterculture of the 1960s to adopt the drug as their own.

Marijuana became closely intertwined with the counterculture. The hippies were mostly smoking leaf that was low in THC (since the trichomes are concentrated on the buds). And, even if they could find buds to smoke, the strains themselves produced less THC since they had yet to be subjected to decades of intensive underground breeding. Nonetheless, getting high became a way of finding intellectual independence from the mainstream of American society much as it had been for the beat writers. Having marijuana, smoking marijuana, sharing marijuana was the norm for many. And when the hippies decided that they wanted to get in touch with their agrarian roots, they brought marijuana with them.

The back-to-the-land movement swept across the United States in the 1960s and 1970s. Communities such as Drop City in

Colorado, started by a group of artists in 1965, and The Farm in Tennessee, begun in 1971, became well-known national symbols for the movement and helped to inspire others to start communities in just about every state. In 1970 Alicia Bay Laurel self-published her book, *Living on the Earth*, about her experiences on Wheeler Ranch in Northern California. A year later, it was picked up by Random House, reviewed in *The New York Times Book Review*, and helped popularize the movement.

At the time, people all across the country were uprooting themselves and moving to these often remote and isolated communities says Tim Miller, chairman of the religious studies department at the University of Kansas and author of *The 60s Communes: Hippies and Beyond*. Miller, who interviewed over 500 people who lived in these communities for his book, says the back-to-the-landers of the 1960s and 70s were young and idealistic and interested in self-sufficiency and small-scale, organic agriculture. "Most of these people were single or without children," Miller says. "They were pretty flexible and at a point in their lives where they were free to move with a lot of fluidity." Most stayed for just a short time—a few years or even just months, but some managed to set down roots for a lifetime.

Pebbles Trippet, a long-time medical marijuana activist who lives in Mendocino County, says that many of the people who moved to these communities left San Francisco because of a sudden change in the city's Haight-Ashbury neighborhood, which had been flooded with hippies during and following the 1967 Summer of Love. But by 1970 things had changed. Marijuana and LSD, which were prevalent in the early years of the hippie scene there, were now being overtaken by heroin and cocaine. The people and the mood changed and many left.

Trippet came to San Francisco in 1969 and quickly made her

way to Mendocino. "I was cold and cashless and wanted to be on the land," she says. In the summer of 1970 many hippies moved from Haight-Ashbury to a campground off the Navarro River in Mendocino where they stayed for a summer. She and a friend had heard about a women's commune and they stayed there for some time. "The gentle, peaceful, anti-war approach had turned sour in San Francisco and we came up the Mendocino coast to be part of what we thought was going to be some measure of personal freedom and affordable lifestyle," she says.

The reality is that many who tried their hand at living on the land quickly found that the simple, rural life they imagined was much tougher than they thought. According to Trippet, "Everything was pretty much raw. You cut your own firewood; everyone lived in cabins. Unless you had money or jobs, you were doomed not to survive." The back-to-the-landers, most of whom had never lived or worked on a farm, had no idea how demanding that life is. "What a simple romantic idea to go out there and grow food and live in peace and harmony with everyone," Miller says. "But to this day it is a hard life to be a farmer. Very few communities really made a living farming." Some communities survived thanks to donations from wealthy benefactors interested in the cause or from the trust funds of participants or the assets of those who joined in the case of those groups that were truly communal, Miller says.

Other communities found a cash crop that was increasingly in demand as more people began to experiment with smoking marijuana across the country. "Income from cannabis helped us survive," says Trippet. "Those who grew garlic as the primary staple of the community did not survive. Those who grew grass as well as garlic did survive, at least for a period of time."

To some people, growing their own marijuana fit in perfectly with the do-it-yourself ethos of the back-to-the-land movement. "The fact that we could grow, I mean, why buy it?" asks one former back-to-the-lander, Otter. (Since he is often identified with one particular community, Otter asked that I not use his real name in order to protect the group's identity.) He moved to one of the many back-to-the-land communities here with his wife and stepdaughter in 1977. "We wanted to make it on our own, like making wine or brewing beer instead of buying it at a store. There is something about it—whether it is a success or failure, it's up to you and you stand behind it with pride."

Otter says one person in his community who called himself Night Eagle (people took new names when they moved to this community) was the resident expert. People traded goods or services with him for seeds and he'd show them the basics of how to germinate seeds, and plant and grow cannabis. That was important, says Otter: "Like so many people, we were fresh out of the city. We had no experience in gardening. This was a whole new world."

Otter germinated the seeds in water and then kept them in a damp paper towel for a few days until small roots appeared. He was instructed to put the strongest seedlings into a peat soil pellet—a hockey-puck-sized disc of peat—and then plant it. He used to stay up nights getting high and watching the plants. All around him his friends' and neighbors' plants were growing like mad. Some plants topped six feet tall. His, however, never got more than a foot or two tall. He got a tiny harvest out of his while his neighbors pulled in pounds of marijuana. Otter could not figure out what had gone wrong. When he uprooted his plants, he came face to face with his mistake: he had never removed the metal mesh on the bottom of the peat pellets. The mesh had stifled the growth of the roots so his plants never had a chance. "It was such a disaster. We were the laughingstock of the community," Otter tells me. "You just have to laugh at yourself."

Though everyone feared getting arrested, a much more real and constant problem for growers throughout the region was theft. It's not as though growers could call the police if someone stole their marijuana. Otter says those in his community did not steal from each other but that outsiders sometimes stole entire plants. Later they stole just the biggest buds. Eventually thieves were breaking into curing rooms and storage areas to steal trimmed buds ready for sale. As a result, his community, like many in northern California, had to do a lot of its own policing. As harvest time approached, they had a sentry up on a nearby ridge who could see anyone coming from miles away. They had a system of CB radios (once a common security approach among many of these remote marijuana growers) to alert each other if a stranger was on the property. Even so, Otter says his community remained worried that it would always be considered an easy target for local thieves. Together, the community decided to try a little intimidation of their own. Every year the nearby town had a Thanksgiving turkey shoot. One year the community sent its best shooters to the contest. "We wanted to blow away the hippie-pacifist stereotype so we sent down our best marksmen and won some prizes in the turkey shoot," Otter says. "It sent a subtle message not to mess with us; we were armed and dangerous."

With so much worry about getting busted and getting ripped off, growers rarely talked to outsiders about what they did and how they did it. They shared information about growing techniques, what kind of nutrients they added to their soil, curing approaches and other elements of the trade only among those they worked with. They had seed connections like Night Eagle who often acted as hubs of information sharing. Growers often partnered with other growers to share upfront costs and labor and hired helpers who eventually became independent growers. Trimmers were sometimes brought in to trim the crop. Each of these groups of associates was tenuously connected to other such groups through social connections or through knowing a dealer. But few people ever talked to those outside of their communities about their trade in much detail. As a result, many of these areas became very isolated. They each had their own seed connections, growing and curing techniques passed from one person to the next. That slowed down the transfer of knowledge between growers.

One community might have a wonderful strain or a better breeding technique but it might never get out to a wider group of people; if it did, it might take years for the ideas to travel from one group of growers to the next. This isolation also meant that marijuana grown in one place was often completely different than that grown just a few miles away, thus leading to an increasing diversity in the plant as every group of growers was developing their own seed stock. This was long before consumers fetishized particular strains. Buyers, and certainly their street-level clients, had no idea what strain of marijuana they were smoking and the growers had little idea of what they were growing. "We had local favorites, like, oh we had Big Wig. I don't know if Big Wig is anywhere else," says Sean. "There might have been talk of seeds from Amsterdam, but who could know for sure if that is where they really came from."

Over the years people developed various organic soil mixes as well as growing techniques to help them boost productivity. For these growers, adding chemical fertilizer or pesticide was never an option. Just about everyone in Sean's neighborhood took their organic ethos seriously. They had no intention of harming the environment to get high or earn money. But their learning curve was hampered by fear. Anything you could not remember from one season to the next was simply lost. "You don't keep a piece of paper that says a word. It goes in the fire," Sean tells me. "You don't keep that stuff around. There are stories of people who do and they get busted and their land is taken away because they've got all the records."

This isolation also had an effect on what was likely the most important development in how the plant is grown. Up until the mid to late 1970s, there could be a hundred seeds in a bag of marijuana. Smokers had to pick through their marijuana to remove the seeds. In addition, letting the plants get pollinated and go to seed reduces it potency. When a female plant is pollinated, it stops growing flowers and instead puts its energy into producing seeds and then it dies. It also halts resin production, resulting in less THC.

California growers began figuring out sometime in the mid to late 1970s that if you kept the males away from the females, they would not get pollinated. And if they did not go to seed, the buds would grow much larger and continue producing THC-laden trichomes. This product is known as sinsemilla, Spanish for "without seeds," and is what everyone smokes today. But back in the 1970s it was a revolutionary development.

And it is one that took quite a bit of time to become widespread knowledge, in part because of the culture of silence that surrounded the plant. Individual growers often stumbled on this by chance. Sean says that growers in his neighborhood had figured out how to cultivate sinsemilla sometime in the mid to late

1970s. Ty, a second-generation marijuana grower who grew up in southern Humboldt (and asked that I use only this name to identify him), remembers when people started growing sinsemilla there. "We had a neighbor who knew about growing sinsemilla," he says. "And at the same time others that just had a single plant found out about it too. All of a sudden they realized that wow, there were no seeds," he says. Suddenly, what they were growing was far more potent than anything they had produced before. Many people all over the region were either finding this out through trial and error or learning about it through the slow trickle of communication between growers. Even experts on cultivation sometimes worked for years before finding out about it. Mel Frank, who wrote the most comprehensive early guide to growing marijuana, began cultivating the plant in New York in 1968, but did not learn about growing sinsemilla until he came to California seven years later. The leap to growing sinsemilla would eventually help to create a viable cannabis industry in California, one where marijuana would eventually sell for enough to support an entire region.

With the promise of a real income more and more people started to grow for profit here in the early 1980s, resulting in increased law enforcement flyovers. To avoid detection, growers began planting their crops under heavier and heavier tree cover to disguise them. But the plants growing in the shade yielded less and less marijuana. Despite their best efforts, theft remained a problem too. Just as growers everywhere were innovating to find their own solutions to problems and developing new approaches to growing and breeding, someone here came up with a novel solution: Grow marijuana in trees rather than under them. The idea certainly made sense. It would be easier to hide the crop 40 feet up in a California live oak than scattered around on the ground beneath the branches. And, with some creative pruning, growers could get more sunlight to the plants in a tree without risking growing in the open. Law enforcement flying over in a plane or helicopter and thieves on the ground would likely miss marijuana plants growing in the leafy canopy of a tree.

Finding a site to grow in a tree was not easy. Live oaks and madrone trees, with their long, fat branches and leaf color similar to a range of strains of cannabis plants, were preferred. But not just any tree would do. These plants had to be watered and since there was no electricity, pumps were never an option. Growers had to find trees that were close to higher ground so a water barrel could be buried uphill from the trees ensuring that there would be enough pressure in the feeder lines to get water up the trunk of the trees to the plants. Paul says that you also had to get the plants up high enough in a tree that someone could not just climb up there on their own to get it. Trees without low branches were key. Water lines would be buried in the ground and they sometimes used tiny eighth-inch diameter tubes to make the lines harder to see as they snaked up the branches to the plant. Each hose had a timer on it and the hose had to be coated with tanglefoot, a sticky paste, to keep thirsty squirrels and other animals from biting through the line. Sean tended many of these grows when he was young. He and his father and later his wife would haul 10-gallon pots 40 feet up into the trees and tie them to the trunk with bailing wire. They pulled moss off the tree to place around each pot to camouflage it. Then they had to haul up the soil. Using a pole saw they would cut away an opening in the canopy so the plant could have at least some direct sun. It was hard, laborious work. "I was really in shape when we were growing in trees," Sean says.

Paul and Sean had plants in about 25 trees on their property, usually two plants per tree. With the increased sunlight they got from their new positions high in the trees these plants would yield anywhere from a half to three-quarters of a pound per plant compared to just a few ounces per plant grown in the shade on the ground. "I was going up in the tree once a week, having to balance while walking out on the limb carrying buckets and a pole saw 40 feet up in the air," he says. But it worked. The crops drew less attention from the air and theft fell off dramatically.

Throughout the 1980s and later, growing all over Northern California only got more lucrative. As the Reagan administration increased its law enforcement efforts the wholesale price of high-quality marijuana skyrocketed—reaching as much as $4000 a pound according to those growing at the time. At the same time the people who moved back to the land a decade earlier were getting older. Many of them now had children and homes. Some of the growers decided to go back to school. Subsistence farming was unlikely to pay these bills. Meanwhile, the world had changed around them. Paul's neighborhood and others like it were founded on the ideals of the 1960s. But by the time Ronald Reagan became president, America was a very different place. The hippies had morphed into the "Me Generation." Selfishness and gaudy displays of wealth had taken the place of peace, love, and community. "It was like the end of the world didn't happen the way they expected it to," Sean says of his parents and their friends. "All of a sudden these hippies who had these great ideals were like, 'oh my God we went off in the wrong direction.'"

Some marijuana growers made up for that by growing a lot of plants and bringing in large sums of money. Sean says a few of them got reputations for being selfish—especially if these larger growers flaunted their income in any way. "There was a disillusionment process that occurred in tandem with the pot culture coming in," says Sean about the early 1980s. "Some people really thought 'oh those pot growers, they have it so easy.'" In reality, he says, even the small-scale growing that he does is a lot of work, involves significant risk, and provides only a modest income.

Paul says that he did not ever grow to survive. He works in a legal local industry and earns a good income. He grew to have money for home improvements and to head to sunnier climates during the winter. "Growing becomes like a gambling addiction," Sean says, about himself and those he knows. There are times when he wants to get out of growing. With prices down thanks to the glut of growers drawn here by the medical market, the money is so bad now that it is hardly worth the effort, he says. But, whenever he thinks they are getting ahead enough to quit, they are drawn back in by a bad crop, an unexpected expense, or any number of financial needs. Like anyone facing mounting expenses in a poor economy, they are doing what they know how to do to make ends meet. "If I can only get one more crop, a couple of more harvests, I can take care of this and that. People funnel the money into their homes and businesses, into their retirement accounts. People become more and more dependent on their income from marijuana," he tells me. "It becomes a way of life."

3 GROWING TAKES OFF

On a drizzly, early summer morning I follow a white, mud-spattered Toyota pickup truck out of Laytonville, a tiny strip of a town at the very northern edge of Mendocino County. The truck takes a right off Route 101 onto Spyrock Road, a narrow, unmarked road that I would never have noticed on my own. Tagging along behind the truck, I switchback up on an increasingly narrow dirt road, rising through the morning fog. In breaks in the fog, I catch glimpses of the surrounding mountains covered in brittle, brown grass, dotted with deep-green live oaks. The hillside falls away at absurdly steep angles. Massive redwood trees fill the valleys below and forested mountains recede in the distance. The trees, the mountains, the rivers, the entire landscape here is immense, outsized in a way that dwarfs the people living in it. Though we're just a few miles from the highway that connects this community to San Francisco three hours south of here, this place feels utterly remote, an easy place to hide away.

We bounce over rutted dirt roads for nearly a half an hour, occasionally passing driveways blocked by a large, metal gates. This far out, where I haven't seen another person or building for miles, one would think that privacy and security were the last things people would worry about. Yet those concerns seem to be a priority here. Without even leaving the car, I can feel the insular paranoia of this community.

The pickup pulls off the main road and the driver leans out the window to enter a code into a box next to one of these metal gates. After it opens, we plunge down a narrow, potholed road and turn again at another fork where he gets out and opens a combination lock on a fat, metal chain that secures another gate. I follow him until the road dead-ends at a two-story house shaped like an octagon. Tom hops out of the pickup truck. He's a thin man with close-cropped hair, a stubbly beard, and the tanned, lined face of someone who has spent much of his life working out-side. He's been growing marijuana up on this ridge since 1986 (and asks that I not use his last name).

Next to the driveway, in what is essentially his front yard, doz-ens of marijuana plants are growing in plain view. Some are in gallon pots lined up against the barn, waiting to get transplanted. Others have already been transplanted into the massive pots that will hold them until they mature. As Tom and I walk over to the plants, we're hit with the unmistakable earthy, skunky smell of marijuana. Tom walks into the midst of about 15 plants, each growing in a pot that he makes using chicken wire to create a frame that is then lined with ground cloth. Each pot holds about 350 gallons of soil and is about five feet in diameter. Tom has learned over time that cannabis plants have wide, shallow root systems, so the wider the pot, the larger the plants will grow and the more buds it will produce. "This one is Sour Diesel," he says touching the long spindly leaf of a three-foot-tall plant. "It does well indoors and outdoors," he says. He points out a few more strains—OG Kush, Green Crack. Sour Diesel and OG Kush are among the most popular strains on the market and easy to sell. "This one's tearing it up," he says pointing out a particularly large Green Crack plant.

Spyrock Road is one of the better-known growing communities in northern California. People started coming up here as part of the back-to-the-land movement in the 1970s and by the time Tom arrived in 1986, everyone on the mountain and all the members of their families were involved in some aspect of growing, processing, and selling cannabis. "Spyrock is one of the greats," Tom tells me. "It's one of the only places where everyone up here is growing, and they have been forever."

Before moving here, Tom was living in Los Angeles. He had been buying marijuana from the boyfriend of a family member. The boyfriend told Tom that he was growing marijuana up in Mendocino and offered Tom, then a 16-year-old high school dropout, a job growing marijuana for him. With few other prospects that he could see, Tom jumped at the chance.

"When I got here I was fortunate enough to sit down with the old guard," he tells me. Tom met a grower he calls the Mayor of the Mountain, who had arrived here from Detroit with a dozen women in a school bus. "All the old brothers who'd been up here forever, they heard Charlie Manson was on the mountain and they went down there to go shoot him up," says Tom. "Instead they wound up becoming best of friends. He was a very powerful conversationalist, he got into people's souls." The Mayor, who died a few years ago, and the other old-timers had been growing marijuana for over a decade by the time Tom showed up. They had learned a lot about growing and breeding, lessons they were happy to pass along.

Tom and I sit in a second-floor room in his octagonal house. His is a nicely constructed building, particularly when compared to many off-the-grid homes I've seen that often have a slapped-together quality. Tom's house feels as solid as any vacation home. Stacks of DVDs line a shelf above us. Downstairs there is a full-size refrigerator and a full kitchen. His sister is busy whipping up a batch of hummus for us. Tom is a bit nervous and, despite the early hour, downs a few beers and smokes a joint while we talk. (He later explains that he has autism and is terrified about meeting new people—the alcohol and marijuana help him relax. It's also part of the reason that he has chosen to live and work in such an isolated place.) He tells me he's never spoken to a reporter before. Given the two and a half decades that he's been steeped in the illegal marijuana business, that is understandable. Tom is dressed in corduroys, a zip-up hoodie, and flip-flops. The outfit makes him look far more laid back than he is. Tom talks and walks fast, a man with direction and little time for idle chatter.

After two years, Tom had saved enough to buy his own property—a place that he calls the old dentist's cabin because, he says, it belonged to the Grateful Dead's dentist and marijuana supplier. Back then a lot of locals traveled to Afghanistan and Pakistan and returned with their pockets full of seeds—indicas that Tom calls broad leaves. These indicas were acclimated to high altitude and a growing season similar to Northern California's (where Tom lives is just a few degrees north of the northern reaches of Afghanistan and Pakistan). Growers also began crossing these early-flowering indicas with the lanky and high-THC Mexican, Colombian, and Hawaiian sativas that they had been growing for some time to create hybrids that produced high-yielding plants that could be harvested in the early fall. These hybrid plants did well here, much better than the Thai plants that some attempted to grow. Those sativas have a much longer flowering cycle because they are adapted to the warm, long growing season near the equator. "Try to grow some of the Thai seeds and you'd wind up with pictures of 20-foot-tall sativa plants with snow all over them," Tom says with a laugh. "That would be your Christmas card—just send that out and forget about harvesting."

The early years of large-scale growing from the late 1970s until law enforcement really cracked down in the early 1980s were a kind of golden time that the older growers waxed nostalgic about to Tom. Police were spotting for grows using airplanes that move far too quickly and at such a high altitude that they would not notice anything except huge fields in full sun. All growers had to do was keep their plants near forested areas in partial sun and spread out the plants. As long as you didn't grow in the middle of a field like you were planting a vegetable garden, you'd be fine. With an increasing number of cannabis strains bred for the local growing season and little attention from law enforcement, growers here flourished. "There were about five years of glory days," says Tom.

Those glory days were the culmination of decades of increasing marijuana use from the jazz clubs in the 1930s and 1940s to the hippie scene in the 1960s and later. Back then, most marijuana was smuggled in over the border and though some people did grow in small amounts here, marijuana didn't really take off as a cash crop here until the late 1970s at the earliest. There are plenty of theories about why it took off when it did. Some point to paraquat. In the mid 1970s, using helicopters provided by the US government, the Mexican government began spraying marijuana fields with paraquat, a toxic herbicide that can cause pulmonary fibrosis if ingested. The US government warned that smoking marijuana contaminated with paraquat could cause irreversible lung damage though it's unclear how much herbicide would be on the marijuana that made it to the United States. The press coverage resulted in a panic among users, who were concerned that they were being poisoned by their marijuana. That likely put a bit of a dent in the market for Mexican marijuana and increased the demand for a homegrown product. But it's unclear how widespread concern about potentially toxic marijuana was among smokers. In 1988, the US government started spraying paraquat on crops grown on private land and other herbicides on crops grown on public land here at home. There is not much evidence to indicate that the spraying dampened demand for domestically grown marijuana.

Others say that it was simply a matter of following the path of least resistance. As pressure built on drug smugglers, it was just less risky to grow it here. Phillip, a former drug runner (who asked that I not use his real name), says that in the 1970s he brought lots of marijuana over the border from Mexico. He took off the bed of his 1959 Ford Ranchero—a car with a pickup bed in the back—to create a false bottom, hiding hundreds of pounds of marijuana at a time. He added stiffer air shock absorbers so that law enforcement would not notice the car riding low under the additional weight. Eventually, he says, customs caught on. Later he began smuggling much larger amounts of marijuana on the east coast. Airplanes would drop bales of marijuana that were equipped with homing devices off the coast of Georgia. He and other smugglers found the bales and retrieved them with high-speed boats. But over time, he says, there were so many busts (Phillip himself was eventually arrested but never convicted) that less marijuana was coming into the United States from overseas. With supply short, prices rose.

In addition to pressuring smugglers, the United States began to focus on the exporting countries, particularly Jamaica. With a large population of Rastafarians who use marijuana as part of their religious practice, the drug was a deep-rooted part of the Jamaican culture. And a lot of Jamaican marijuana was finding its way to the United States. In the mid 1970s the Jamaican government, under pressure from the US government, allowed the American Drug Enforcement Agency to begin operations in its country. From the mid 1970s on, there was increasing pressure on those bringing in marijuana from Mexico, Jamaica, and elsewhere.

Then the marijuana market underwent a radical change, says Tom. In the mid to late 1970s Mexican marijuana sold for between $100 to $300 a pound wholesale to dealers according to Tom, a price that was so low, there was really no incentive to take the risk and expend the effort to grow marijuana domestically. Earlier in the decade, US soldiers serving in Vietnam were bringing back seeds and marijuana from Southeast Asia that was incredibly strong compared to most of what was being smuggled in from Mexico. It wasn't long before smugglers started finding ways to bring in high-potency marijuana from Thailand and that changed the entire market. This marijuana was an order of magnitude better than most of the Mexican and Colombian cannabis that was commonly available. Such a high-quality product commanded a higher price, which was important because it cost a lot more to smuggle marijuana from Thailand than it did to sneak it across the border from Mexico. Smugglers had to pay off customs and shipping officials. They had to bring huge quantities across the Pacific. Marijuana from Thailand, Tom says, sold for $1800 a pound. And given its superior quality, smokers were willing to pay for it. Thai marijuana had suddenly created a market for a powerful and very expensive product.

Thai marijuana hit the market about when the first generation of back-to-the-landers were learning to grow sinsemilla, the

THC-rich, unpollinated, seedless buds. Sinsemilla from northern California's most potent strains could sell for as much as the imported marijuana from Thailand and without the risk and overhead of an international smuggling operation. With real money to be made, more and more people were interested in growing. "When people started to realize they could get the same price for their homegrown sinsemilla as they were getting for the Thai marijuana, now you've got every damn dealer and smuggler and their brother flocking up to the hills to start growing," says Tom. "That is what made it financially doable."

There was money to be made, and for many locals it was one of the few options for making a living in this remote area. Ty, the southern Humboldt grower, began growing on his own in 1980 when he was just 18 years old. By that time, many of his friends were already growing and, for a teenager with few local options for making a living, the success that his friends were having was an incredible incentive to begin growing himself. "I had friends here that bought their first piece of property when they were still in high school. They were driving a Mercedes to school instead of an old Chevelle," Ty says. "There was definitely a sense that there was money to be made if you go that way." And, Ty says, with the timber and fishing industries in decline locally there were few options for employment and none that would pay as well. "I didn't even know what else there was to do here," he says.

At first Ty grew on his parents' property, then later with partners. For a few years he partnered with a friend to grow on that person's mother's property in southeastern Humboldt County. He and his growing partner lived in an old Army tent with a wooden floor. "We were roughing it, but it was a good time," says Ty.

Others were drawn to the area for the prospect of growing here. Lawrence Ringo, who owns the Southern Humboldt Seed

Collective, was one of those who arrived in the 1970s. Ringo started smoking marijuana when he was 14 years old. "I just love the way it makes me feel," he says. "It takes a lot of the cloudy shit out of my head. If you want to excel in life, the first rule is don't sweat the small shit. Pot helps me not sweat the small shit. I find that space where time just kind of stops, I'm not in a hurry or anything."

Ringo began growing when he was 15 years old and living in Arroyo Grande, a small town about 80 miles up the coast from Santa Barbara. Ringo told me that he found a pistol and a large gold ring with a sapphire in it inscribed to Duke. Once he learned that Duke was a leader of the local chapter of the Hell's Angels, Ringo decided to return what he'd found, in part to meet one of the Hell's Angels. Duke was so happy to have his ring and gun back that he asked Ringo what he wanted. The young Ringo pointed to a large marijuana plant growing out in the yard and said that he wanted to learn how to grow that. Duke gave Ringo his first seeds and taught him how to grow them. "He showed me what the buds looked like right at peak time when they were done, how to harvest, he showed me how to pollinate, everything. It was very cool." Months later, when Ringo's mother found a dozen plants in her backyard, she didn't think it was quite so cool. She kicked him out of the house.

By the latter half of the 1970s, Ringo was living in the mountains near Santa Cruz and growing a few plants. He started hitch-hiking up to Humboldt to visit a friend to play music and take psychedelic drugs. The marijuana he bought here was powerful and cheap and Ringo found himself hooked on the place and the experience. In 1980 when he was 23, Ringo and his wife bought his property with a small down payment on a remote ridge in southern Humboldt County. It was former sheep ranch that had been subdivided into 40-acre plots. And, he says, the realtor who had subdivided the property knew exactly what people would be doing up here. Every parcel had a dirt road leading to it and its own spring. "He took us up in a little Cessna, over all this beautiful land," says Ringo. "The couple of people who were growing had like 500-plant gardens and when we flew over the realtor said, 'Here's your competition.'"

Ringo's early years in Humboldt were a kind of grower's paradise. There was little interference from law enforcement and people could essentially grow as much as they chose to. "You could come up here and grow your 100, 150 pounds until about 1984 without any hassle," says Ringo. "We always had partners so we split the money four ways. We paid off the land in three years."

With the land paid off and three young children to provide for, Ringo kept growing and was able to put his money into the property, building his home, adding solar panels and other infrastructure. Eventually he left, working building clean rooms for a high-tech company in Santa Cruz and Colorado, spending a dozen years away from the area before returning. But wherever he went, he still put a few marijuana plants in the ground to grow his own crop.

Lots of people, like Ringo, began to grow just for personal use. After all, cannabis is a plant and just about anyone can stick a few seeds in the ground. It doesn't mean that they'll get a worthwhile harvest, but it's simple enough to try. Tom Alexander, who would go on to publish *Sinsemilla Tips*, a popular marijuana growing magazine that lasted from 1980 to 1991, put his first crop in on Cape Cod in 1974 before moving to Oregon and growing there. In backyards, on decks and balconies, across the country, people tried their hand at growing marijuana. People were obviously interested in the plant and there was a real thirst for knowledge. Many of these amateur cultivators learned their trade thanks to a book by Mel Frank and Ed Rosenthal published in 1978 called *Marijuana Grower's Guide Deluxe Edition.* Frank (his pen name) lives in Los Angeles' steep hills. He's got two rambunctious dogs, a home filled with artwork created by his wife and their friends. You'd be hard pressed to guess that this fit, graying baby boomer is one of those responsible for the widespread cultivation of marijuana in the United States. Downstairs, his obsession is a little easier to discern. On his desk he has a microscope with a bud under the lens and a small tray with more buds laid out. He's experimenting with a new technique for taking pictures through a microscope that allows greater depth of field so he can take better quality photographs for a new book he's working on. In his closet he has a small indoor grow of about six plants. Outside, he has a few more plants that he tries to keep hidden out of deference to his neighbor who works in law enforcement. "He seems like a very nice guy," Frank tells me. "I don't want to put him in an uncomfortable position of having to look down and see a plant, and then have him go through the turmoil of thinking, 'What am I going to do? It's my neighbor.'" An angry radical Frank is not.

During his stint in the Navy, Frank was an electronics technician on a ship patrolling the North Atlantic. When he got out in 1967, he moved to New York City. He found a room in a huge rent-stabilized apartment and it wasn't long before Frank was smoking marijuana. The marijuana at the time, he says, was about half seeds—sometimes many hundreds in a bag. He started growing some of those seeds in 1968. His apartment had a long bank of windows that got great light. He set up a large table there and built growing trays from wood stolen from construction sites. He used a combination of natural light augmented with fluorescent lights. At first the plants never came into bud. He was keeping them under lights for far too long—up to 16 hours a day. Then he started cutting back on the hours of fluorescent light from 16 down to 12 or 13. He didn't know that marijuana plants only flower when the days get shorter. He was just muddling his way through by trial and error. By 1970 he had 100 plants growing in the apartment. Frank was also tinkering with growing outside in upstate New York and had some incredible successes there, despite its shorter growing season. He has photos of plots thick with towering marijuana plants. He shows me one old black-and-white photo of a marijuana plant growing next to a large pine tree. The plant appears to be at least 20 feet tall.

In 1970, Frank published an article in the New York Flyer insert of *Rolling Stone* about how to grow. Ed Rosenthal, another avid grower, got in touch with Frank and asked him to write a grow guide with him. At first Frank wasn't interested. But Rosenthal, who at the time was selling small indoor grow kits, was persistent. "Ed basically bugged me for a year to write the book and I did it almost to get rid of him," Frank says. While growing, working on the book, and working for the phone company, Frank went to night school to get a degree in biology with a focus on botany. That radically boosted his understanding of the cannabis plant as well as techniques for growing and breeding. Meanwhile Rosenthal worked on pitching the idea to independent publishers until he found one that would take the project. In 1974 the pair published a short 128-page book. Shortly after that Frank got much more serious about botany and interested in publishing an in-depth guide to the plant.

The pair moved to California in 1975 and Frank continued his detailed and meticulous research on the plant. When the

Marijuana Grower's Guide came out in 1978, it was one of the first grow guides and certainly the most rigorous at the time (Frank says proudly that the book had over 230 entries in the bibliography). It received a brief but glowing review in *The New York Times*, which called the book, "an extremely clear and interesting essay on practical horticulture, as accessible a study of a single plant, at this high level of seriousness, as one is likely to find." The endorsement boosted the book's distribution and sales. Though exact sales figures are not available, Frank says that it has likely sold over 800,000 copies since it was first published and remains among the most thorough and easy to understand guides written on the plant.

Frank and Rosenthal's book, along with a few others—Rob Clarke's *Marijuana Botany* (Tom says that he's read this book about 30 times) and Jorge Cervantes' *Indoor Marijuana Horticulture* and subsequent books—taught generations of growers how to cultivate marijuana, indoors and out, and how to breed and produce seeds. These books are all incredible successes. But back in the 1970s, even finding a publisher for these books was not easy—it took Rosenthal years to find one. With the exception of a rare mention in the mainstream media, these books only found their audience thanks to the outlets and networks developed by the underground press.

David Tatelman, founder of the Homestead Book Company, was a key figure in helping these authors spread their cannabis knowledge. He had owned an independent counterculture bookstore in Tacoma, Washington, in 1970 but that quickly failed. He then started distributing underground comics like those by Robert Crumb. About that time he met a writer named Dave Fleming, who had written an early growing guide. Tatelman figured that it would appeal to the buyers and customers of the same head shops and counterculture bookstores as the comics. He started distributing Fleming's book, along with Frank's and later Cervantes', sometimes driving himself from store to store with a car loaded down with books. In some cases the booming sales of these books kept these independent shops afloat and helped Tatelman create a business distributing these titles. "These guides were very important to small bookstores," says Tatelman.

Not long after Frank and Rosenthal moved to California, they bought a house in the hills high above Oakland and began breeding plants there together. Frank was an avid seed collector and had seeds from all over the globe—from Congo and Nigeria to Sumatra, Pakistan, China, and Colombia—so he had a remarkable stock to work with. Growers who had read their book started tracking them down through word of mouth. And once word got out about their breeding operation and seed collection, they found themselves hounded for seeds. Frank was happy to hand them out but could only produce so many given their relatively small and somewhat urban home. Without even meaning to, Frank and Rosenthal quickly became not only a source for information about growing techniques, but a key source for seeds for northern California growers. And those growers inevitably bred the resulting plants from Frank's stock with their own plants, helping put Frank's genetics into the strains that have come to dominate the marijuana grown in the region. "I gave away, I can't tell you how many seeds I gave away during the 70s and early 80s," says Frank. "I gave away thousands, thousands and thousands of seeds."

As more and more people started knocking on Frank's door and growing began to take off in California, law enforcement began to take notice. So much marijuana was being grown in the state that politicians in the conservative and intolerant Reagan era could no longer overlook it. Marijuana cultivation became a hot political issue. In the early 1980s, George Deukmejian, who was then California's Attorney General, invited the press to watch him don a flak jacket and take part in a Mendocino County marijuana bust. (Deukmejian later served as California's governor, from 1983 to 1991.)

In 1983, the Campaign Against Marijuana Planting, or CAMP, an organization comprised of federal, state, and local law enforcement agencies was formed with the sole purpose of finding and uprooting marijuana gardens and prosecuting growers. One of the Spyrock growers, Tom, told me that in the beginning, CAMP really didn't understand what it was doing. "The first year they came in April or May and whacked down all these plants that were like two feet tall," Tom says. "All the growers looked at each other and put in another crop and still had a great year." But CAMP soon figured out an effective system. It adjusted its efforts to coincide with the harvest and took a very heavy-handed approach. "When they came in they were going for the throat," Tom says. "They would shoot up water tanks, chop your water lines, and make it difficult to get right back on it. They would confiscate everything. I've watched them haul off ATV's. Instead of cannabis, they had people's toys in the bottom of a net beneath the helicopter." Michelle Gregory, a spokesperson for the California Department of Justice, which runs CAMP, says that the agency did not seize property but that its local law enforcement partners did. The agency, she says, is still vigilant about destroying the infrastructure needed to grow in these remote areas, sometimes following buried water lines for miles to find the source and destroy the lines.

The possibility of losing your crop, of having your property confiscated, and of getting arrested was very real. "When a helicopter flew over, my knees would get weak," Tom says. "I'd run for the woods and I'd be afraid for my life." This constant law enforcement presence was enough to drive out many of the back-to-the-landers who were just dabbling with growing. According to Tom, "A lot of them just said, 'this is just too much.'" They stopped growing and moved away. With CAMP destroying so much of the crop and increasing the risk, the wholesale price of marijuana doubled from about $2000 a pound to about $4000 a pound.

CAMP has only gotten more aggressive with time. In its first year it seized and destroyed 63,000 plants. By the end of the decade it was seizing three times that amount each year. In 2010 CAMP seized 4.3 million plants. "We had a war with them for seven or eight years," says Ringo. He began hiding plants in the woods elsewhere. He says that military UH-1 helicopters would buzz the property regularly. Law enforcement agents would routinely show up expecting to search his homestead. "They would take everything from you if you weren't around," says Ringo. "But if you stood your ground they would have to come talk to you. It blew their whole plan out of the water." Ringo was used to law enforcement bullying. His father was a sheriff's deputy and, he says, the most intimidating person he ever met. Ringo was fairly comfortable going toe to toe with the police and was well aware of his rights. "I'd tell them, 'Go ahead and shoot me, I am not a pot grower,'" he says, and then laughs at the fib. "Well, I didn't have any pot here."

Growers began moving their plants deeper and deeper into the trees. Tom, who like most growers put his plants in the ground under trees, as opposed to Sean and Paul who actually put theirs up in the tree branches, says that properties with lots of manzanita trees were suddenly coveted. The manzanita, which is native to hot, dry climates, turns its leaves sideways so they are vertical to help reduce the amount of direct sunlight that hits the leaves so they do not dry out. The manzanita is perfect camouflage for cannabis plants. It obscures marijuana plants grown in the ground beneath it from those zipping by in a helicopter while still letting light through to the plants growing beneath its canopy.

According to Tom, CAMP's early fall raids also pushed growers to try to bring their crops in earlier. Instead of simply growing full year outdoor crops, many began planting light deprivation crops. These crops were grown outside, usually under large metal hoops. Each day, after 12 hours of sunlight, growers would pull tarps or dark plastic over the hoops, plunging the plants into early darkness. That would force them to flower early so they could be harvested before the CAMP helicopters started their raids in early fall. Tom also pushed to wrap up his breeding operations by late summer so he could destroy many of the unwanted plants before there was any risk of arrest. Tom says that growers figured out that the CAMP officers were interested in making the largest busts they could so they could generate big headlines. CAMP's Gregory says that the agency was out to make the biggest impact so it wanted to target its efforts at the largest grows it could find. That often meant skipping over the smaller ones they found. Part of that is driven by federal minimum sentencing guidelines requiring that those convicted of growing over 999 plants serve 10 years in prison. Those convicted of growing between 99 and 998 plants must serve five years. Those who grew fewer than 99 plants on any single piece of property would not trigger minimum federal sentencing guidelines and would likely be left alone. To keep plant counts low, growers often put their plants on many different parcels, sometimes partnering with friends on their properties or buying several properties themselves to grow on or, in some cases, even growing in the woods on public land (something that was frowned upon then and still is today) or private timberland. CAMP was likely to ignore small plots of 70 or 80 plants and the growers could maximize the number of plants they grew with less risk of losing the crop or being arrested.

For these growers, smaller was better. "We had to stay small so as not to appear like we were trying to bite off more than we could chew. You just don't want to grow too much more than your neighbors," says Tom. Despite the fear and the tension that built up as harvest approached and flyovers began, Tom says neighbors up on Spyrock Rd. tried to stay civil with each other. "We'd try really hard not to point fingers up here," Tom says. "Everybody's got their shit and live and let live, you know. That's why these people were up here in the first place, to try and cultivate that type of society."

Despite his best efforts, Tom lost one full crop to CAMP in the 1990s though he was not arrested—not an uncommon experience since, according to Gregory, the agency is focused on eradication, not on building cases against growers. Gregory says an arrest is viewed as a bonus, not as a primary goal. With so many growers here who were all under the constant threat of losing everything, Tom says the community on Spyrock Road really came together. "Some of my worst years were my best," Tom tells me. As Tom and other growers told me, growing marijuana created tight bonds between neighbors and in some ways accentuated some of the higher ideals of the back-to-the-land movement. Not that there were not betrayals where people gave up friends and neighbors under the threat of prosecution—that certainly happened. And growers can be incredibly egotistical about their abilities. But often, when the threat of arrest loomed, it brought out the best in people, Tom says. "I'd get CAMPed on" and lose an entire crop to CAMP officials "and a friend shows up and slaps $100,000 on the desk and I go buy this new piece of property with that down. It saved my ass," Tom says. "It's a tight, tight family, a good one, a hell of a model community in my opinion."

And despite all the attention from law enforcement, people here made good money, sometimes a lot of it. A six-figure profit was the norm, Tom says. In a good year when prices were at their peak, a grower could clear a quarter million, even half a million dollars if they really pushed the number of plants they were willing to risk growing. By the end of the season growers had a lot of cash lying around. Tom would often give money or marijuana to growers who had been busted to help cover their legal fees; he was happy to help out people he didn't know just as he had been helped out by a friend. But other growers found more esoteric ways to spend their income, Tom says. They would buy humanitarian supplies for the Burmese freedom fighters or travel up the Amazon River to do obscure drugs with indigenous tribes. Another, he says, was convinced that humans originated in Scandinavia, not Africa, so he put all the proceeds from growing into funding archeological digs there. "Pot growers are nuts, man," Tom tells me. "But as far as risk and reward goes, this is the best job on the planet."

4 BREEDERS CHANGE EVERYTHING

The southern Humboldt grower, Ty, lives in an off-the-grid home hidden down a maze of dirt roads and tucked beneath a wooded hillside. One afternoon, he takes me for a walk through his marijuana garden. We duck under the boughs of a pine tree and walk down a narrow path and, almost without realizing it, I find myself standing in the midst of his collection of plants. Ty, a small-scale breeder who loves tinkering, shows me a plant he's bred that has a bright purple stem. It's half Kush and half Blueberry. The purple stem is not necessarily common in either of the strains, Ty explains. This plant came from a strain that produced well in the shade but the purple stem was buried deep in the genetic profile of the plant. He says that of the hundred seeds he started, only five had purple stems. He liked the purple look so he selected for that. Another nearby plant that was bred from the same males has a similar purple hue but not as pronounced. "There is definitely something back in the plant's history," Ty says.

He shows me a taller, lanky sativa-dominant plant, a cross between Snow Cap and Jack Herer, a strain named after the author and cannabis activist, that he calls Jack Frost. Ty decided to work with this particular plant to see if it could be a viable strain to produce. One of his reasons was that it reminded him of a strain of particularly sweet-smelling marijuana that had been grown locally in the 1970s. He may wind up crossing his Jack Frost with Sour Diesel to create his own Headband strain (Headband is Sour Diesel crossed with Jack Herer). Ty shows me another female plant with a purple stem. "This one had great odor and smokability," he says. "This was the best of the group so I'm calling it Bright Lights Kush after a type of kale that has a multi-colored stem."

Cannabis names don't follow much rhyme or reason. There is no commonly used convention for naming, no regulator or association that will penalize people for refusing to follow its rules. People name plants as they choose. Sometimes the names are chosen to reflect some of the strains in its makeup. But even that can be tough given that there has been so little record keeping of any kind, particularly among strains that were developed some time ago. Since nearly all of today's strains were bred from some of these older strains, attempts at tracing back a plant's lineage beyond a few generations often ends with some origin story about people meeting at a Grateful Dead show or a bar. Even obvious names that you might think give some indication of a plant's history can be incredibly misleading. Kush, for example, usually refers to indicas from Pakistan and Afghanistan, a reference to the Hindu Kush region. But OG Kush (the OG is usually said to refer to it being Ocean Grown since it was developed in southern California, though it is sometimes also said to stand for Original Gangster) is primarily sativa with only a bit of indica in its background, so even the Kush name applied to one of the most popular strains is a misnomer. Ty, for example, incorporates the names of other vegetables he likes. Other breeders just give their strains whatever name suits them; sometimes that name tags along when someone else develops a derivative from it, sometimes not.

Ty has been breeding plants ever since he began growing. He enjoys playing with combinations, bringing out less-dominant, interesting traits. When he is happy with a strain, he grows what are known as starts, young plants that are already sexed (the males have been removed) for buyers who want female plants that are a couple of feet tall and ready to be planted in the ground. These he sells primarily to growers he knows in the area, via word of mouth. Ty is not a big-time breeder. He does not have a seed company. He is not like a lot of breeders who push only for high yield and ever-higher THC levels. Instead, he is looking for something more personally appealing in how he manipulates the plant. "I go for quality and a certain beauty of the plant," he says. "How it smokes, and how it smells. I'm kind of a snob when it comes to flavors and smells."

Breeding marijuana is often a challenge because breeders cannot grow huge numbers of plants, which would be the best way to find the highest quality iterations of the desired traits and the most vigorous plants. The more individual plants growers have to choose from, the better they will do. With only a few dozen plants to work with, it's hard to view the full range of genetic possibilities, especially when some traits might only appear in one in a hundred plants or a few in a thousand. Shantibaba, one of the top breeders in Holland in the 1990s who now co-owns Mr. Nice Seed Bank (who asked that I identify him by this name), says that when he developed Super Silver Haze, a popular strain that won multiple cannabis competitions, it came from a single plant picked from a thousand that he grew to maturity. If he had grown fewer plants, he may not have found the one with the characteristics that led to Super Silver Haze. "There certainly was something special there," he tells me. Shantibaba's process for breeding is remarkably labor intensive and expensive given that he grows and discards so many plants. He often had 30 or more projects in one stage or another of the breeding process at any given time. "There is a lot of trial and error," he says. "You bring loads of plants into flower and think about what they might combine with well." Often he just relies on his intuition and decades of experience to decide what to discard and what to move forward with: "It is just an automatic understanding when I look at a plant. I can feel it. I can't explain it, but I know what is good and what isn't." With Super Silver Haze, he says that anyone would have been happy with just about any of the 999 plants that he discarded. "But when you are breeding," he says, "You are looking for the greatest progeny of the next generation."

Some lines of the plant became inbred because breeders took shortcuts with their strains, combining plants that had too many genetic similarities and not working with enough plants. Ty says that in the 1980s when he and others grew large numbers of female plants under trees (growers had to cultivate more individual plants because the yield per plant was very low under tree cover) it was easier to breed than it is today because you could grow such large numbers of plants through to their flowering cycle to determine the quality of the marijuana and the yield. Flowers on the best of those plants could be pollinated by placing a bag of pollen over the flowers so no females would be inadvertently pollinated. The seeds could be grown out the following year to determine which had the best yield and produced the best cannabis. Cuttings of the best plants could be held onto as a mother for use in breeding the following year.

Though Ty has no seed company and is not well known like other breeders, his constant efforts to breed over decades out of a sheer interest in the process and the outcome is important to understanding how marijuana got to be where it is today. He is part of a vast decentralized network of people who enjoy manipulating the plant, creating new strains with different desirable characteristics, and customizing strains for their own needs: plants that grow well in particular conditions like shade or fog or shortened growing seasons and those with more THC. Amateur breeders, primarily in Amsterdam and California but certainly elsewhere too, have been taking their own routes towards strains that they hoped would be desirable, pushing up the value of their own crops and of the seeds they could easily produce. "We got what, a million guys on the job in California?" asks Tom, the grower and breeder from Spyrock Road. "Ten percent of them—100,000 might save the best clones. Those clones get passed around and vetted and eventually the cream rises to the top. That is what separates California, particularly northern California, from any place else on the planet. There are a million guys on the job and a million guys looking for the same thing—somebody is going to come up with some pretty good stuff."

Breeders like Tom and Ty learned much from friends and family members, but such breeders also owe much to the pioneering grow and breeding guide authors like Mel Frank. Inside of his Los Angeles home office, Frank is sitting in front of a computer monitor and walking me through his photographs of the cannabis plant. He shows me detailed images taken through a microscope that magnify the resinous droplets of cannabinoids in the trichomes, the long, wavy, tendril-like stigmas of the female flower, and the almost cantaloupe-like dangly male cannabis flower. As he explains, since cannabis is wind pollinated, the plant does not create large or brightly colored flowers like those plants that must attract insects or birds in order to transfer pollen and reproduce. Instead the female cannabis flowers are tightly packed at the end of stems, making them more accessible to pollen moving on the breeze. A male plant produces over 500 million grains of pollen compared to several thousand female flowers on a typical plant because the chance of a tiny grain of pollen landing on a stigma in the wild is slim. Pollination is a numbers game. As the male flower blooms, the sides of the flower pull back to reveal what looks like a tiny bunch of bananas. These are anthers that hold the pollen. They open up from the bottom as if they are being unzipped to release the pollen grains. "Here I actually caught the pollen coming out," Frank says, excitedly showing me an image of the pollen falling from the flower. He has taken thousands of magnified photographs of the plant over the years and seems incapable of becoming bored with the images. He remains end-lessly curious about the plant, excited about the tiniest revela-tions. Like a great college professor, he is still fascinated by his subject decades into his career. "When you see them hanging like this, by this little filament, you think the wind comes and they sway in the breeze, but they don't," he announces. "They vibrate. They vibrate like crazy."

When pollen lands on the long stigmas that appear on the buds of the female plant, the pollen grain forms a tube that works its way down the stigma to the egg or ovule at the stigma's base. Two sperm cells travel to the egg and form the embryo and endo-sperm, which becomes the food source for the embryo. Each of the thousands of eggs on a plant has to be fertilized by a sepa-rate grain of pollen to produce a seed. Pollen from any number of males, some from many miles away depending on the wind and luck, can pollinate a single female plant.

With this type of heterosexual reproduction, each seed carries the genes of both parents. And those genes combine differently every time, making each individual plant different from its parents and different from each other.

Breeders, however, have no interest in fostering the kind of diversity that shows up in the wild. They want to select for certain advantageous traits and be able to reliably produce uniform plants—an identifiable strain of cannabis. So, they choose particular males and females to breed that have those traits. Breeders have a wide variety of techniques that they use to pollinate a plant. Some capture pollen by placing a plastic bag over the male flower and shaking it to get it to release the pollen. They then put that plastic bag over the female flower to pollinate it. Some capture the pollen and then paint it on the female with a brush. Just about any means of transferring the pollen from the male plant to the female bud will do.

The mechanics of pollination may be simple—it's part of what has led to so much diversity in the plant, but like anything, doing it well, and doing it well over time, is no simple task. Great breeding takes organization, patience, and an almost irrational obsession with the plant. "Great breeders are all nuts," says grow guide author Jorge Cervantes. "They are all wacko. There is a gene or something; there is something different."

When breeders cross two cannabis plants, particularly the hybridized plants on the market today, some of which are the result of breeding multiple hybrids with each other, they will usually find that they get an incredible range of diversity in plants. The key to effective breeding is to find two stabilized strains to work with. Stabilized strains are those that have been selectively inbred through multiple generations until all their offspring exhibit consistency in desirable characteristics such as potency, flavor, size or yield. Breeders select plants with the qualities they want, such as height, yield, the type of high it produces, or a particular color, or smell. The more plants breeders start with, the more variety in traits they are likely to find to choose from. They then focus on the plants with the traits they like and stabilize the strain.

The best way to do this is to breed groups of plants that express the similar desired characteristics until the strain is stable. But that process is time consuming and requires breeders to grow many plants, increasing their risk of detection and imprisonment if they are caught. Instead, breeders can perform what breeders of marijuana and of legal plants call backcrossing, in which they cross the progeny that has particular traits they are looking for with the parent plant that expresses those traits. Each generation that is backcrossed will express less variation than the previous one. It is another way to try to fix certain traits or bring out dominant traits that exist in the parent that are not as well defined in the offspring. And it allows growers to shortcut growing enormous numbers of plants, which is often impractical and risky.

Once breeders have what they refer to as a true breeding plant, one that produces little diversity in its first generation, they can breed it with another true breeding plant with different complementary characteristics to make seeds. These seeds will produce plants that uniformly express the desired characteristics in the first generation—what is known as the F1 generation. There should be no diversity. Nearly all commercial seeds are F1 seeds. Plants in this first generation will have a mid range of traits of the parents. For example, if you bred a small and a tall plant you'd primarily get a medium height plant in the F1 generation. The plant will also be about 25 percent more vigorous than the parents. Marijuana breeders may have been winging much of their approach to growing the plant, rediscovering basic well-understood techniques like growing from cuttings, but when it comes to breeding, they have incorporated the Mendelian techniques and language used by those in legal agriculture.

Some breeders, however, see the F1 generation as just the beginning of the breeding process. These breeders are not simply looking for a mid range, they are hoping to get a plant that expresses the extreme characteristics of each parent—say high yield and high THC, not mid-level THC and mid-level yield. In explaining the process to me, Tom uses the example of breeding Haze, a tall and wispy but very powerful sativa with Deep Chunk, which is a short, broad indica with dense resinous buds. A breeder would not want the resulting plant to express the kind of mid-parent traits commonly found in the F1 generation. "You don't want a mid-sized plant," Tom says. "What you want is a big, giant plant, tall and broad with very potent resinous buds—you want the best of both plants."

In order to do that, breeders have to move past the first or F1 generation. All plants tend to express their recessive traits in the second or F2 generation and it is these F2 plants that have a wide range of diversity. Because of the way it breeds, cannabis plants can express an exceptionally broad range of diversity in the F2 generation. By breeding two of the F1 plants of mid-range height, breeders find that the F2 generation will yield a spectrum of plants, the majority of which express the dominant trait. If tallness is dominant, the majority of plants would be tall and then some smaller percentage would have varying heights. If the breeders plant enough seeds, they will find that the extremes in this generation will likely accentuate these characteristics even more than in the parents—some F2 plant will be even taller than their parents. Other traits not seen at all might rise to the surface like the purple in Ty's plants. "The breeding of new lines begins with the F2," says Tom. "You set aside the elite individual from that generation and create your new line from there."

With the F2 generation, breeders can start selecting these extreme characteristics for breeding whether it is high THC, a purple hue, or whatever characteristic the breeder desires. Once he has a plant he is happy with, the breeder can then stabilize that strain to create a new F1 generation from which to create seeds.

Most grow guides have sections devoted to breeding. Frank and Rosenthal's *Marijuana Grower's Guide* is no exception. Almost as soon as Frank began growing marijuana he began amassing a vast collection of seeds and breeding. In the 1970s Frank was getting seeds from Afghanistan, very pungent skunky weed, and some Durban Poison from South Africa, useful because of its fast maturation time. Frank, like most breeders, wanted to select the most potent plants to breed, but back then there were no labs set up to test for THC levels. So he had to get creative. Frank smoked his own marijuana and had his own impressions of the potency but he wanted a larger sample. He gave his friends numbered joints containing different strains of marijuana and asked them to write up a little report after they smoked each one. He asked them to be as regimented as possible about it—smoke at the same time each day and note how long the high lasts (which he figured was a good indicator of how potent the strain was). But it didn't always work out so well. "One woman wrote, 'well it was a really shitty day and the dog peed in the bed'—This is not a diary," Frank says, still sounding a little annoyed decades later. "I want to know about the dope."

In 1976 Frank and Rosenthal began to breed on a much larger scale. They bought a house in the Oakland hills with a small shed out back. They put in as many windows with frosted glass as they could and covered the inside with reflective material. As we talk, Frank pulls out a stack of yellowing paper—notes from his early years of breeding in Oakland in the late 1970s. Unlike many breeders at the time, Frank kept copious notes despite the risk. He felt that if he was ever put on trial, a jury in liberal-minded Oakland would not convict him since his work was geared towards research and seed production, not growing to sell for profit. He looks at his notes on an Afghani (an indica) and Nigerian crossed with a Hawaiian—both sativa dominant if not full sativas. "The hybrids were just so vigorous, they were so good in every aspect, they were wonderful," says Frank. Another list of seeds that he finds shows strains from Burma, Tibet, China, Thailand, Sumatra, Korea, Indonesia.

The pair had an incredible diversity of plants growing at any given time. "There was a South Indian that I grew that was so sweet that I just wanted to bite it every time I went in the greenhouse," Frank says. "There was the skunkiest skunk you'd ever had." (According to Frank, the skunk odor indicates an indica-dominant strain.) The pair grew everywhere they could think of. "We grew in the attic, we had it in the windows and in the ground in the backyard and in pots. When I think of it, we were pretty outrageous," he says. "My sister came to visit and somebody came in and asked if there was any dope around. She said 'yeah, here,' and pulled some out from under the couch cushion. It was everywhere."

The seeds he and Rosenthal cultivated were the basis for the strains that he passed along to northern California growers and which they, in turn, began crossing as well, coming up with their own hybrids. As, it turns out, Frank's seeds were also used by the early seed companies in Amsterdam that shipped seeds all around the world and made it possible for just about anyone to grow their own marijuana.

In the early 1980s, Dave Watson, one of the pioneers of marijuana growing and breeding, who would go on to become a pivotal figure in the industry, was planning to move to Amsterdam and wanted some seed stock to take with him so he could start anew over there. Frank gave him Afghani #1 and Durban Poison. Watson added them to his collection which included Original Haze, Skunk #1, and Hindu Kush. The seeds in Watson's collection were an important part of the founding of the Amsterdam seed business.

Amsterdam has been a mecca for pot smokers for decades. Though cannabis is technically illegal in Holland and smuggling has always been dealt with harshly, the government has had a long-standing policy of not enforcing the law on small amounts of cannabis. It is essentially acceptable for anyone over the age of 18 to possess up to about an ounce for personal consumption and to grow five plants. Coffee shops that sell marijuana can only keep about a pound on site and can sell no more than five grams to an individual at any one time. Because so many Europeans now go to the Netherlands to buy marijuana, the government began outlawing sales to anyone not from the Netherlands in parts of the country in 2012 and may ban foreigners from buying the drug in Amsterdam in 2013, part of a slow decade-long shift away from its previous open tolerance of the drug. In 1997 the government instituted new rules about growing that imposed jail sentences on anyone growing over 99 plants. As a result many breeders and growers moved elsewhere in Europe. Despite the recent shift, the country's historically tolerant attitude about drug consumption and cultivation helped spur a culture of coffee houses, seed companies, and head shops and attracted growers and breeders throughout the 1980s and 1990s. Amsterdam is home to the Hash, Marihuana and Hemp Museum (admission is free for children). The original High Times Cannabis Cup, an annual celebration of cannabis and a competition for the world's best marijuana, a sort of Super Bowl for pot growers where judges smoke dozens of strains to choose the winner in several categories, was first held there in 1988. Many of the biggest names in marijuana breeding and cultivation from around the world gravitated to this city. But it wasn't always that way.

One of the pioneers, who very early on wanted to turn Amsterdam into the Jamaica of Europe, was Wernard Bruining. He grew up in the former Dutch colony in West Papua, the western half of the island of New Guinea. After relocating to Holland he smoked his first joint when he was 19 and found that he connected much better with the marijuana smokers than with anyone else he was meeting in his new home—their relaxed attitude reminded him of the people from New Guinea. In 1969 he and his housemates began selling hash, a paste made up of the potent trichomes commonly sold in North Africa. "I realized there was a big need for reliable sources for hash and grass," says Bruining. In 1973 he opened the first coffee house in Amsterdam, the Mellow Yellow coffee shop. Buyers could walk in and purchase hash for a set price. "We made scoring accessible to everyone," says Bruining. The Mellow Yellow became so popular that customers lined up out the door to buy.

At the time no one was growing marijuana in Holland. All of the hash and marijuana was being smuggled into the country at significant risk. Just five years after opening, a fire erupted in the Mellow Yellow and it had to be closed down. Bruining, interested in learning more about growing marijuana, decided that he would take a trip to the United States. While in Oregon he met Old Ed Holloway, an early pioneer of growing sinsemilla. Bruining was amazed at the quality and potency of American marijuana and convinced Holloway to come back to the Netherlands. Using seeds that Holloway brought with him from Oregon, the two of them formed The Green Team with the goal of teaching the Dutch to grow high-quality marijuana so it would not need to be smuggled into the country anymore. In 1979 they sold their first crop to The Bulldog, another early coffee shop.

In 1981 Bruining started the Lowland Seed Company, the first company dedicated to distributing cannabis seeds in the Netherlands. He provided buyers with seeds, fertilizers, and an instruction poster—a basic grow-at-home kit. Bruining wanted more people to grow on their own in a self-sufficient way rather than rely on purchasing marijuana from coffee shops. The Green Team also kept growing using Holloway's seeds, which were well suited to Holland's short growing season. But they wanted to be able to boost production and continue to increase quality. In 1984, they invited Ed Rosenthal, Frank's co-author, and Watson, who went by the name Sam the Skunk Man, to come to Amsterdam and help The Green Team.

The Green Team chose to work with Watson rather than Rosenthal because of the quality of his seeds, says Bruining. The Green Team, which was expanding to include more people, tinkered with growing techniques, starting outside, then moving into greenhouses to find the most effective ways to grow via trial and error. They discovered by accident how to clone plants from cuttings, says Bruining. When they went to visit one of their many grow operations, they found that a storm had broken the branches off a number of plants. Bruining, who was hesitant to see the branches just get thrown away, put them in the ground almost as a joke. When he came back a week later, he was surprised to see that some of the branches were still alive and had begun to take root. It was a discovery for them but a common agricultural technique used for hundreds of years on legal crops.

In 1983 they began planting cuttings from the most vigorous, healthy plants, those with the best yield and that produced the most potent marijuana based on their experience smoking it. Eventually, The Green Team wanted to expand to a 50,000-square-foot greenhouse. Bruining decided that such a massive growing operation was not for him. He was far less interested in his own bottom line than he was in promoting the idea of growing and smoking. "My life on this planet is not for the purpose of making a lot of money," he tells me. "I am here to improve this world." In 1985 he started Positronics, the first grow shop in Amsterdam. Bruining had about 50 strains of seeds and clones to work with and customers brought in more from all around the world. He bred some new ones but mostly worked with what he had on hand, selecting the best plants to harvest seeds from.

By 1985, the seed had been planted in Amsterdam, so to speak. There was a massive local supply of cannabis available for the burgeoning coffee shop industry. Thanks to the ingenuity of some of the best growers and breeders from the United States and Holland, the marijuana grown here could now rival that from anywhere in the world. The seed stock that launched the industry here provided an incredible base. As the city became known as a hub for marijuana smokers, seed collectors from around the world stopped in, dropping off interesting seeds they had collected, picking up new seeds to bring home with them to experiment with and cross with local varieties, thus developing entirely new strains of their own.

The seeds that Watson brought with him from California would become part of the foundation of the cannabis industry in Holland. In the introduction to *The Cannabible*, a book by Jason King, Rob Clarke writes that 80 percent of the 150 strains that were being sold by Dutch seed banks in 2000 contained some genetics from strains brought there from California in the early 1980s. Skunk #1 was particularly important, says Ed Rosenthal, Frank's co-author. The strain was potent and produced a large amount of buds so outdoor growers appreciated it. It also produced well indoors and was easy to manage in smaller environments under artificial light so indoor growers flocked to it. "It's like the Big Boy tomato," says Rosenthal. "It changed the way that people grew and it opened the door for other varieties to come."

In the early 1980s an Australian named Neville Schoenmaker arrived in Holland. He started a massive indoor grow in his home, which came to be known as The Cannabis Castle. And he began the first mail-order marijuana seed company, The Seed Bank. With that he sparked an industry. Over the years more and more breeders and growers gravitated to Holland, developing hybrid strains geared towards indoor growing, which was taking off at the time. This provided an easy way for growers all over the world to obtain high-quality seeds. Thanks to Schoenmaker, the other breeders in Amsterdam, and the vision of Bruining, access to seeds became democratized. Growers no longer needed a connection to a breeder, they could simply open the pages of *High Times*, check out an ad, and order their seeds.

Over the last several decades breeders in Amsterdam as well as those in California and elsewhere have added tremendous diversity to the plant. Thanks to these seed companies, just about anyone can purchase seeds and begin breeding, says Kenny, the co-owner of Trichome Technologies, a grower who has been featured in numerous cannabis magazines and was voted the best producer in the history of *High Times*. "Any kid can buy strains, breed them, start stabilizing them and come up with the next new thing," says Kenny (who asked that I only use his first name). "Even two kids in the middle of nowhere who know damn near nothing."

And that capability has completely changed the plant. Breeders began by creating hybrids of indicas and sativas. These hybrids were then bred with other hybrids and on and on. Popular strains like OG Kush, Sour Diesel, Blueberry, various purples and others found their way into dozens, even hundreds of strains. "Between 1985 and 2005 cannabis probably went through the largest and most rapid transformation in the history of the species," Kenny says. It's a transformation that continues today. Breeders in the United States and Spain catering to the medical market have created more strains since 2006 than the breeders in Amsterdam did in two decades of work, according to Cervantes—although many are only slight variations from others. But that important boom in diversity has not been without its problems.

Unlike breeding programs for any other plant that is cultivated on a large scale in industrialized countries, cannabis breeding is totally unregulated. No one determines what OG Kush really is and there is no penalty for someone slapping a popular name on a random hybrid (except for the potential scorn of angry customers on cannabis message boards). Since cannabis is illegal, breeders cannot claim legal rights to their plant strains. The fast-growing seed and clone business is highly competitive. Buyers seek out hot new hybrids developed from old favorites. With high demand for these hybrids, seed companies, dispensaries, growers, and dealers all rush to get these seeds, clones, and cannabis to market. Unfortunately, that speed works against quality breeding programs that can demand years to properly isolate and stabilize a strain—far more time than the market allows. Seeds are often rushed to market before the strain is properly stabilized; as a consequence, the plants grown from these seeds will often be quite different from one another. Problems associated with inbreeding can crop up too.

A Canadian breeder who goes by the name Chimera, who has an academic background in neuroscience as well as biotechnology and plant breeding and has been selling seeds for over 15 years, says that some seeds and clones available today are inbred and that inbred plants tend to be weaker. Problematic traits often get carried from one generation to the next alongside the traits that breeders were hoping to reproduce. If you think of the cannabis plant's 10 chromosomes as, say, 10 avenue blocks in a city, Chimera says, and you are selecting for a trait in a building at 100 4th Avenue, you are going to also wind up selecting those traits in the neighboring "buildings" as well. And if you keep breeding the plant over and over with its parent, the offspring will also have the same neighboring characteristics that will get passed along too. Those traits, which may turn out to be undesirable, will continue to be amplified as they are passed along from generation to generation (just as the traits you are hoping to enhance are amplified as they are passed along) and the inbred plant will eventually become weaker and yield less. In the same way, traits can be bred out of the plant, much like CBD was bred out. Pest or mold resistance or other qualities may have also been sacrificed over the years of pushing for high-yielding THC-rich strains.

According to Chimera, the way to avoid the problems associated with quick-turnaround inbreeding is to work with larger numbers of plants. Instead of selecting two individuals with desirable characteristics, breeders should be selecting 20 percent of say, 1000 plants with desirable characteristics and breeding those with each other so that in the next generation there may be 30 percent that express the traits you are looking for, and so on. These plants, Chimera says, will likely be more robust since they have a greater diversity to start with so deficiencies are likely to be more spread out among the population without sacrificing the particular traits the breeder is looking for. "Breeders should be slowly moving a population towards a given goal," he advises. "The reality is that real improvements take time."

Breeders have often been driven by making a quick buck. With no uniform regulation or oversight, it is simply easier, faster, and more profitable to create hybrids using fewer plants, taking as few steps as possible. Chimera is concerned that the explosion of quick-turnaround breeding—demonstrated by the fact that the number of seed companies has ballooned with the medical marijuana markets in California and Colorado—will harm the plant over time. Because the plant is illegal, there are no centralized cannabis seed banks that store seeds from rare and historic strains. Untold numbers of genetic lines have been destroyed by the police in raids. Much of what is available to work with is limited to what one can find on the market or through connections. "With the method that we are using now for breeding, with short-term goals, in about 40 years we are going to see some real problems with genetic diversity," Chimera says. "Though I have a duty to give everyone what they want from the plant, I also have a duty to myself and my own work and the species to leave the plant in a genetically healthy state so that when someone comes along after me they have a healthy population in which they can make further progress."

Strains that are hybrids of the indica and sativa subspecies have been central to the recreational market. They are so common that there are few pure sativa or pure indica strains to be found anywhere. For example, on Harborside's website in late 2011, the dispensary listed 35 strains of cannabis for sale. Only three of those were pure indicas and none were pure sativas. The seed hunters who scour the globe for landrace plants are having a harder time finding them. Eradication efforts have caused many landrace plants to disappear completely; others are in areas such as Afghanistan and parts of Africa that are war-ravaged and difficult to get to. So breeders have little choice but to work with the popular hybrids that are commonly smoked today. "Hybrids are great," says Tom. "That is where it is at—one plant covering for another's faults, but it is really important to be able to repeat the process. Unless you put a real importance on keeping the pure lines pure, then you just can't go back and revisit the scenario."

Few breeders have been able to hang onto these pure lines, or if they have, they never release the seeds to the public. Frank says that he was long frustrated that the Amsterdam seed companies created and sold seeds for hybrid strains only. The strains they created were admittedly wonderful—very potent and perfectly bred for indoor growing—but, he says, they were all very similar. There was none of the diversity that he remembers from his own growing experiments in the 70s. The seed companies know that releasing the pure lines would be bad for business. In an unregulated market, competitors could quickly and easily create copycat hybrids that would compete with a breeder's existing stock. Stabilizing a strain is incredibly hard work and no one wants to just give away the fruits of their labor. And, creating great strains from these vigorous pure lines can often be easy since they are so different from one another. The Southern Humboldt Seed Collective breeder, Lawrence Ringo, remembers when he first obtained pure sativa and pure indica seeds in the early 1980s. "They have been growing the same indica in some places for generations. The buds on them were just insane—purple, really gorgeous stuff," says Ringo. "Then I crossed it with my Acapulco Gold and the next year I had plants that were 15 feet tall and 10 feet wide. I was like holy shit."

Ringo is once again growing Acapulco Gold. "Having those original strains again, it's very important because everything has been so overbred, the genetics are so washed out, it's hard to get something pure again because everything has been crossed and crossed for decades," he says. Many of those hybrids have similar strains in their lineage so crossing them does not help breeders find traits that are different and complementary in the way that the pure sativas and indicas can complement one another. Instead, says Tom, breeders need access to some of those pure indicas and sativas. Without them, quality breeding becomes much tougher.

Tom has tried to preserve the pure lines, holding on to seeds and growing plants to create new seed stock. He is growing out lots of pure indica—strains from Afghanistan and northern India that were some of the early ones to come to northern California. He's looking for promising plants to begin breeding even though they may not be that popular. Tom views it as his responsibility to the plant to maintain these pure strains. No one is making Tom do this. He is doing it simply because he feels it is important. The fact that Tom is doing this work, investing his time and money, simply because he feels it is important, is one of the strengths of this underground, totally unregulated business. Many breeders do take advantage of the wild-west environment, injecting poor genetics into the marketplace and the species. But others develop a commitment to the plant and take on an almost conservationist role totally outside of the needs of commerce simply because it is important to the species and to the generations of breeders to come.

"Tom is a purist, a type of person that is important to any species of plant," says Chimera. "There has to be someone who maintains the pure lines and develops these pure lines and tries to improve them. They might not grow as big or be as potent but if no one maintains the pure lines, where would we be?"

5 CANNABIS MOVES INDOORS

Marijuana grower, breeder, and activist Ken Estes drives me through an industrial part of East Oakland in his white Toyota sedan. We stop at a driveway that is blocked by an eight-foot-tall metal gate on rollers. Using a remote control, Estes opens the gate and we drive through. A young man, one of Estes' employees, removes Estes' wheelchair from the back of the car, helps him into it, and then wheels him into the building.

Inside, three men are sitting around trimming buds to the hum of massive exhaust fans overhead. It's a poorly lit, dingy, and open space that feels a bit like a sweat shop or a place to stash stolen shipments of flat-screen TVs. It's a far cry from the bucolic mountaintops of Mendocino. Estes, who wears a blue button-down shirt and jeans, looks like a tanned California entrepreneur. He's enthusiastic, quick to laugh, and has an open, friendly way about him. It's quite easy to imagine him owning a tanning salon (he owned two before getting into growing full time), and a bit weird to see him at the trimming table in this desolate ware-house smoking marijuana. He does so in a quick, almost method-ical fashion (he smokes for pain relief, to encourage sleep, and to enhance his appetite) devoid of the social ease with which many of the rural northern growers I had met usually smoked.

After taking three hits from the bong, he leads me down a long hallway. Around the corner, the room opens up. A space the size of a basketball court is filled with two-foot-tall marijuana plants. The room is so large and dimly lit that it's hard to see how far back the plants actually go. Overhead, 100 high-pressure sodium lights are suspended from the ceiling on a pulley system so they can be raised and lowered. That way they can remain close to the top of the leafy plant canopy and simply be raised as the plants grow taller. The strength of light diminishes dramati-cally as it gets further from the source—a light placed one foot from a plant is nine times more powerful than a light three feet from a plant. This system allows the maximum possible light strength at all stages of growth. Overhead, shiny foil ducting runs from one light to the next—a system for drawing the heat generated by the bulbs away before it leaves the light box. This helps to keep the room from getting too hot and minimizes the air-conditioning bills.

"This is all Grand Daddy Purp," Estes says, pointing to the plants. This strain put him on the map in the cannabis com-munity when he began selling it in 2003. It's been referenced in the film *Pineapple Express*. The rapper Lil Wayne mentioned it in one of his songs. It's a pure indica, so the plant is short and bushy, perfect for indoor growing. It produces bright-purple buds with a fruity flavor when smoked and is known for an ener-getic high, something unusual for indicas. These plants are still in the vegetative stage so they are only about two feet tall and are getting 18 hours of continuous light a day. The temperature and humidity in this room are constantly monitored and automatically adjusted to optimum levels. During the last two weeks before harvest Estes drops the temperature down to 55 degrees, causing the buds to turn the deep purple that they are known for. Unlike Marco, who recirculates his air and adds in carbon dioxide, Estes pumps in fresh air and exhausts the existing oxygen-rich air through charcoal filters that scrub it of its telltale odor. All of these systems are controlled by computer. "I automate as much as I can," says Estes.

These plants are all potted in dirt using organic nutrients and methods—a relatively new approach for indoor growers. Indoor cannabis cultivation really took off in the 1980s and 1990s in part in reaction to the helicopter raids on outdoor growers and in part because it allowed people to grow free of scrutiny anywhere regardless of the climate. Back then, Estes says, most people grew hydroponically, without dirt in a neutral medium like coconut husks or perlite or various mixes of water and air. It is a more efficient way to deliver nutrients to the plants than growing in soil and it pushes the plant to yield more of its THC-rich flowers more quickly. It's still a popular way to grow. But hydroponic growing on this scale can be risky. If a line clogs, a timer burns out, or a pump fails, a grower can lose an entire crop in a matter of days. Soil is more forgiving. Moisture and nutrients remain in the soil for long periods of time so if someone forgets to water for a few days, nothing will die. (Estes' gardeners water the plants by hand rather than automating it because, he says, in such a large grow it can be easy to miss plants that are having trouble. This way, gardeners must check each plant individually when they are watering.) Growing in soil, however, presents its own challenges. Soil can contain mold spores and different pathogens that could potentially ruin a crop too. Estes sprays his plants with neem oil, which is produced from the seed and fruit of the neem tree. It is commonly used as an organic pesticide for many legal crops to fight an array of insects including aphids and white flies. "I think if you are diligent and stay on top of your plants you can catch that stuff," Estes says. And, Estes says, he has found that growing in soil produces a more potent and better-tasting bud. "I want those qualities more than I want yield," he says.

Right now Estes' plants are bunched up, about 12 to a light, and portions of the room are empty. Since the plants are still small, he can fit more under each light and run fewer lights to save energy. When the plants begin to flower in about a week, Estes says he'll spread them out, about four to a light or 400 total plants. When he harvests, Estes will get about 150 pounds of dried and cured buds from this room (a pound and a half of dried marijuana per light is considered a solid yield, particularly for Grand Daddy Purple which yields less per plant than other strains). Estes harvests about four times a year. Six hundred pounds of marijuana a year sounds like a lot. But, Estes says, he is barely able to keep up with demand. "I don't even have enough to supply the patients at my dispensary," Estes tells me. "The demand is so large and my supply is so small, even with a hundred lights."

That is in stark contrast to the kind of declining market that the outdoor growers are seeing. Estes has a few advantages. He runs two dispensaries where he distributes his Grand Daddy Purple strain so he does not have to sell to other dispensaries at low wholesale prices; instead, he earns much higher retail prices for his marijuana. Because he is growing indoors, there is a higher demand for his marijuana—it simply looks more appealing than the marijuana grown outdoors and that look is what consumers have come to expect. And he has managed to create a tremendous amount of buzz about this and other strains he has. His Bay 11 strain won top awards at the Medical Cannabis Cup in San Francisco in 2011. At that event, his Grand Daddy Purple booth was mobbed all afternoon—you had to wait in line just to walk around the crowd waiting in line in front of it. And, like some popular strains, it has an origin story, something that never hurts sales either. Estes tells me that after helping out a member of a Native American tribe in northern California who was losing his home to the bank, the tribe's spiritual leader gave him the Grand Daddy Purple mother plant as a gift. In front of us the branches of the plants are already starting to turn an uneven pale purple. "Once the lights come on you can see more purple," Estes says. "And once it starts flowering, the purple comes everywhere."

Estes was first drawn into marijuana cultivation for its medical properties. He broke his neck in a motorcycle accident when he was a teenager and was paralyzed from the waist down. He wasn't eating or sleeping and was on a range of pain relievers. Then he tried smoking marijuana to relieve his symptoms. "For the first time in six months I felt calm and relaxed," Estes tells me. "I slept all night and woke up the next day and ate breakfast."

As a result of the accident, Estes lost the use of his legs and some mobility in his hands and arms. Undeterred, he went to college and later opened a tanning, nail, and hair salon. He also started growing marijuana. "I was growing it in bedrooms, little storage sheds, along fences," he says, adding that doing this alone while in a wheelchair was challenging work. "This stuff worked and I wanted to grow my own." In the early 1990s, Estes sold his half of the tanning business, joined ranks with medical marijuana activists in San Francisco, and began growing full time.

Thanks to the technology developed over decades, Estes and others like him have been growing marijuana here in the Bay Area and in places all over the world where the climate or urban environment would not naturally support the plant. And they have been able to grow year-round, often right under the nose of authorities without getting arrested. Breeders have developed strains that are shorter and squat rather than rangy and tall and that complete their flowering cycle in about 60 days. Indoor growers can produce four or so crops in a single year. Companies that cater to this market have been innovating new systems—lights, fans, high-tech aeroponic grow systems, and automated atmospheric controls—all of which allow plants to be grown anywhere you can imagine putting them, be it in a closet, basement, garage, or warehouse. And these systems allow growers to produce marijuana in optimum conditions, pushing for the highest yield of picture-perfect buds every time. All the uncertainty that outdoor growers face due to rain, wind, temperature, humidity, and shade is eliminated. Indoor growers control every aspect of the climate and can set it perfectly every time. "I love the technology," Estes tells me as he sits in his wheelchair surveying his new grow facility. "I don't know how I would have done this before."

One of the first to take up the cause of indoor growing was Jorge Cervantes. Originally from a small town in eastern Oregon, Cervantes began smoking marijuana when he was 17. He moved to Mexico to go to college where he discovered high-quality marijuana. Though Mexican cannabis is often derided as poor quality, that is more often the result of poor treatment of the buds after harvest—harsh drying, packing into bricks for shipment, even getting soaked with soda to keep the bricks together—than the genetic makeup of the plant. The Mexicans, Cervantes says, save the best stuff for themselves. He moved back to the United States a few years later to finish school in Portland, Oregon, where he says he began to grow and got to know others who were growing indoors. "I could see that growing was a good deal," Cervantes says. "I dealt for a few years but would lose all of my money every eight months on a bad deal. There was the fear of being arrested and spending time in jail." In 1980, after seeing friends of his get arrested and under some pressure from his wife who was unhappy about the risk, he started looking for something else to do. Cervantes realized that there was little good information available about all of the indoor growing that he was seeing around him in Oregon. When he pitched the idea of an indoor grow guide to the publishers who had done the well-known guides of the time, he was turned down, told that everything had already been written about marijuana.

Cervantes pushed ahead anyway. He put together a 10-question survey about growing techniques and went out to growers he knew and people they knew. A lot of people turned him away thinking he was an informant, but he persevered, and spoke with over 200 different growers. He learned an incredible amount. "It was a better book because I paid attention to what other people knew," he says. Cervantes wrote, illustrated, and published the book himself. He found a printing press that he could use at night and ran it himself. He collated and even stapled his book together on his own. "I got cramps from running the stapler," Cervantes tells me. "Everyone thought I was nuts. People felt sorry for me."

Since then Cervantes has written six books on growing, many of which have been updated multiple times and has put out four sets of instructional DVDs. His books are published in seven languages. It's rare to find a grower who does not have a copy of one of his books hanging around somewhere. "Everybody gets given Jorge's book by someone," one grower told me when I noticed a copy on the floor in his house. Cervantes has managed to carve a career for himself out of thin air. He is considered among the foremost experts on marijuana cultivation in part because he has never changed his basic approach—talk to lots and lots of growers. In an industry where few people spoke about what they did and how they did it, Cervantes became an important conduit for information from one growing community to another. And he developed an institutional storehouse of understanding about the plant breeding and growing techniques in an industry totally devoid of that kind of centralized knowledge.

Over the years, Cervantes says, indoor growing has gone through many evolutions. In the beginning there were few types of lights available. Most growers just used long-tube fluorescent lights. But they gave off little light and plants had a hard time producing much under their glow. In the 1970s, high-pressure sodium bulbs originally used for streetlights became available to the public. They were much more powerful than standard fluorescents and are still used by growers today. By 1983, when Cervantes' first book came out, ads for powerful metal halide bulbs, also used in streetlights, were published in *High Times* magazine.

Companies were also coming out with grow kits. The high output lights could not just be plugged into the wall. Growers had to have a ballast that moderated the current so the light would not draw too much electricity and overheat—common in high-intensity and fluorescent lamps. This gave companies the opportunity to sell kits—lights, hoods, ballasts, timers all in one—so that indoor growers could get everything they needed in one shipment. In the 1980s the market boomed. Companies sprouted up everywhere, with all sorts of inventions; many of these, Cervantes said, were useless, but some proved to be important and useful.

Entrepreneurs in the cannabis world began looking to mainstream agriculture and discovered one of the techniques that would come to define indoor marijuana cultivation: hydroponic growing. Hydroponic growing took off in the 1980s and companies put together hydroponic grow kits designed for a few plants under a single light. Kenny, the co-owner of Trichome Technologies, bought his first indoor grow kit in 1980 when he was just 13 years old. It was called the Hydropot and consisted of little more than a tray with lava rock and a bubbler to distribute oxygen and nutrients to the plant's roots. "I still have a picture of myself from when I was 13 with the first early hydroponic kit," says Kenny. "Growing took a lot of trial and error, a lot of reading *High Times*."

Hydroponic agriculture is, in the broadest sense, any way of growing that enables plants to absorb water, nutrients, and oxygen through their roots without the use of soil. Plants can grow just fine without soil as long as water, nutrients, and oxygen are delivered on their own. Scientists began experimenting with growing this way in the 19th century, but it wasn't until the 1930s that it was first used in commercial production. Peppers, tomatoes, cucumbers, lettuce, and other high-value vegetables are often grown in greenhouses using hydroponics because it can increase production. Growers can use any number of neutral mediums to hold the root systems—coconut husks, rockwool, perlite, sand, or even air (as long as the roots are shaded from sunlight). In some systems, plants sit in a medium and trays are flooded with water and nutrients. Others use drip lines to deliver a steady stream to plants in pots. In some, like deep-water culture, the roots are submerged in water. Nutrients are added and the water is oxygenated. In nutrient film technique, a stream of water and nutrients trickles over a mat of roots that are exposed to air but not light. There are a number of different approaches but the central idea is to separate the root system from the rest of the plant and cater specifically to what each needs to maximize yield.

The San Francisco grower Marco uses a system called aeroponics to mature his clones. It is essentially a large black box with a few dozen clones poking out from the top. On the visit to his grow room, Marco shows me the system. He turns the pump off and lifts back the lid, which opens up like a suitcase. Inside I see stark white roots dangling down from each of the plants. These clones were cut only 10 days earlier, yet their roots are nearly a foot long and thick, much thicker than one would expect for something that was a branch less than two weeks before. "You get much bigger clones with much bigger roots than you could ever pull off otherwise, and much faster," Marco says. "It works great."

Tiny jets inside the box atomize water under high pressure and spray it onto the roots. This kind of system allows the roots to obtain lots of oxygen, which they need, along with water. The plants above bask under the lights, totally separated from the air and water mix below. I imagine that it's tempting to grow plants all the way through their flowering cycle like this—the yields would certainly be greater and faster. But, Marco says, the pitfalls are too great. "It's very touchy," Marco says. "If a breaker pops, a jet clogs, the cat eats the pump, something happens, then your plants die and they die really fast." For that reason, he limits this particular high-tech approach to the clone stage.

All of this interest in indoor growing and hydroponics came along at just the right time. In the mid 1980s the pioneering growers in Holland were themselves learning to grow indoors and in greenhouses. And by the end of the decade, they were starting to sell the seeds of the plants they had created that were perfectly tailored to this new growing environment. Like the growers in California (many of them came from California), they were growing both indicas and sativas. The indicas that were brought over from Pakistan and Afghanistan were short, broad plants that often did not produce as much as the tall, lanky sativas when grown outdoors. But indicas, it turns out, were much better suited to an indoor growing environment where rooms could not accommodate a 15-foot-tall plant, but could accommodate lots of short, squat plants. With artificial light, the shorter and broader the plant, the better. Since the power of light diminishes so dramatically over distance, a tall plant would get the most powerful light on only the few leaves and flowers at the top. The most powerful light is more evenly distributed on a broad plant. But the breeders in Amsterdam did not want just indicas. They wanted to maintain the energetic high of the sativas too, says Kenny. "The indoor producers, they are really responsible for all of today's hybrids," says Kenny. "The hybrids controlled the height and increased the THC content."

Skunk #1 was among the pivotal strains. It was consistent and potent and grew well indoors and out. However, Cervantes says, it also took a long time to complete its flowering cycle, 10 weeks or more. As breeders got more familiar with growing indoors they realized that if they could shorten the amount of time that it took for the plant to finish flowering, they would use less energy and be able to grow more crops in a year. Unlike those growing outdoors, where high yield per plant is important, indoor growers expect to harvest only a few ounces from each plant. A short flowering cycle would work just fine for those growing a dozen plants under a single light. Other strains like Afghani #1, Northern Lights (originally developed in British Columbia), and other hybrids of sativas and indicas were developed to have shorter flowering cycles and to be shorter, bushier, and much more conducive to indoor growing.

These seed companies popularized the hybrids and began sending them around the world. Hybrids caught on, even with outdoor growers, and started the plant on the path that it remains on today, combining the strengths of both indicas and sativas. These companies opened up the world of hybridized, specialized seeds to home hobbyist growers. Magazines like *High Times* and *Sinsemilla Tips*, as well as Cervantes' grow guide, helped people learn the techniques required for indoor growing. Now someone sitting in his house in a small town in the Midwest could order up a hydroponic grow system, mail order some seeds from Amsterdam, and begin to grow all without ever even talking to another marijuana grower. "Indoor growing opened the door to lots of people—it became more secure and you could do it anywhere," says Cervantes. "It was a huge thing."

Not surprisingly, the government took notice. In 1988 the US DEA began what it called Operation Green Merchant. Rather than target growers as CAMP did, or dealers or smokers, this effort targeted the grow products themselves, via the stores that sold them and the publications that advertised them. As part of the operation, DEA agents went undercover, asking hydroponic store employees how to grow marijuana with the hopes of getting them to incriminate themselves. Agents subpoenaed storeowners to produce lists of their customers. Suspects identified in garden store records were subject to intensive surveillance, including scans of their homes with heat sensing technology and reviews of their electricity bills designed to determine whether or not they were growing. In 1989 the DEA raided hydroponic stores across the country, seizing records and inventory and arresting 440 people including store owners. By 1991 the efforts had led to 1262 arrests, and the eradication of nearly 1000 indoor grows. Agents also seized assets worth $17.5 million.

The pressure on hydroponic stores and manufacturers forced them to stop advertising in magazines like *High Times* and *Sinsemilla Tips*, a move that forced the latter magazine out of business in 1991. The DEA put out an arrest warrant for Neville Schoenmaker, the king of the Amsterdam seed revolution, though he was never extradited to the United States. "Operation Green Merchant ruined the lives of a lot of people," says Tom Alexander, the former publisher of *Sinsemilla Tips*.

The industry, however, did not die out; it just went further underground. For a decade suppliers strictly avoided any mention of cannabis on products designed to grow the plant. However, the market remained and companies found ways to continue marketing and selling their products; this became much easier as the Internet blossomed in the 1990s. Today, Operation Green Merchant is a thing of the past and, at least in certain areas, marketing for cannabis cultivation is in full swing. Walking through a grow store in Humboldt County or Oakland that has shelf after shelf of nutrients like Big Bud, Bud Igniter, and Kushie Kush, it would be difficult to guess that the government once cracked down on these products.

In addition to the pressure put on garden supply stores by the federal government, CAMP was stepping up their efforts in northern California in the late 1980s and 1990s. The constant flyover from helicopters, the raids, and arrests made growing outdoors harder and harder. Plants had to be grown deeper under tree cover every year, which led to the need to grow more and more plants to get the same yield. That, in turn, increased the probability of a long prison sentence in the event of an arrest.

It didn't take long for many of the established outdoor growers in the area to consider indoor growing. Though most of these large-scale outdoor growers were on remote ranches off the grid, it would be simple to rig up generators to run grow lights, ventilation, and climate control systems. The thing is, says Tom, who tried indoor growing briefly, there is no point in having a small indoor grow off the grid. If you have to run a generator, a large generator doesn't use that much more fuel than a small one. If you are going to invest in the space, the equipment, and the fuel, you might as well get your money's worth. "If we have energy, we have a lot of it," says Tom. "There are usually really big grows up here."

A fellow grower, Anthony Sasso, owned three separate ranches on Spyrock Road where Tom lives. Sasso grew up in Mendocino and says growing marijuana was not really a choice, it was the only way to survive. He tried growing his first marijuana plant when he was seven. As a young teenager, he began growing in Jackson State Forest, a 50,000-acre public forest in Mendocino. Growing on public land is frowned upon now due to the large-scale cartel grows that are very unpopular in the area but, Sasso points out, he had little choice if he was going to grow since he had no way to afford his own property at the time. He says that he has always been fanatical about avoiding any sort of pollution from his growing operations, something that has become a growing problem in the area. In the late 1980s visiting Canadian growers showed him and others the basics of indoor growing. In Canada, virtually all of the marijuana is grown indoors and they had been at it for much longer than those in California. The economics of it sounded fantastic to Sasso. "You could harvest up to two pounds a light every 56 days," he tells me, figures that are not impossible depending on the strain but are at the far end of what most growers have told me they can produce indoors.

In addition to power, growers in these remote, off-the-grid ranches needed something to grow marijuana inside of. Some growers built entire houses filled with nothing but grow rooms. But building several houses on multiple properties was expensive. Sasso came up with what he considered to be a better solution: he would literally grow underground. He excavated a massive hole on his property and poured a concrete slab. He placed five shipping containers—two on each side and one across the end so they were configured like a U—on blocks above the slab so he could run ventilation ducts underneath. The shipping containers on either side of the U were set up as grow rooms; the one across the end was for the generator. A long shaft extended from each of the shipping containers connecting them to swamp coolers to control the temperature. He set up air intake and exhaust vents and water and fuel tanks and buried the entire setup. On top of the shipping container that housed the generator was a trap door. Aboveground he built a shed inside of which he sank two posts in the earth to support a steel crossbeam. Using a pulley suspended from this beam and an ATV with a winch, he could lower supplies in a cargo net through the trap door to the shipping container below.

Sasso began by growing lots of small plants, cramming as many as he could under each light. This "sea of green" approach to growing gained popularity in the late 1980s. Sasso could squeeze 40 plants under each light. But with two of these subterranean shipping container grows going at once, he wound up with a lot of plants on hand. Each grow was run off of a 60 kilowatt generator that could operate 30 lights at a time. One room with 30 lights would be on for 12 hours and the other room on for the next 12 hours. Each underground grow had 60 lights. He quickly realized that 40 plants per light would get him a lot of time in prison if he was ever caught. He cut the number in half and found that the plants grew larger and each yielded more buds so he was still producing the same amount of marijuana. Later he found that if he grew six plants to a light the yield was about the same—about a pound and a half or two pounds per light depending on the strain. And that way he kept his total number of plants below 1000, which would trigger a 10-year minimum federal sentence.

Sasso shows me photographs of the inside of the shipping containers. Large plants heavy with buds hang their branches over the edge of tables. Plants that he says grew about three feet tall and several times as wide consume the room. "You had to crawl around to move in there," he says with a laugh. "If you can't see the floor you are doing something right." Sasso tried his hand at breeding as well but most often grew Blueberry, Romulan, Durban Poison, White Widow, Green Crack, and Red Shredder. The plants were so dense and resin-heavy that he tells me that one of his employees who had long dreadlocks went to bed after a day of crawling around among the plants and woke up the following morning with the pillow stuck to the side of his head.

Growing like this incurred significant costs. Beyond the initial costs of the shipping containers and heavy equipment required to build the subterranean complex, and the plants and climate control systems, he had to keep it running. He buried a 10,000-gallon diesel tank near the shipping containers that had to be refilled every eight weeks. Several employees were required to tend the plants; dozens were needed to trim the buds.

The income was remarkable. Sasso says these two underground grows brought in about $2.8 million a year. He spent $800,000 building a backwoods mansion for his wife and children on one ranch. He traveled to Mexico and Hawaii and went skydiving often. "It was a good lifestyle. We had luxury homes, we traveled when we wanted," he says. "But I also worked a lot."

In 2002 it all came crashing down. Someone informed on Sasso and he was charged with growing marijuana not only in Mendocino but in Oregon too. He pleaded guilty, was sentenced to 14 years in federal prison, and is eligible to get out in 2015. When we meet, in a prison in California's central valley, Sasso shows me a book of laminated photos of his growing operation and tells me that the worst part has been his separation from his children. "That has been a living hell," he says. Their names are tattooed on his arms in colorful gothic script. As for his growing career, that is over. He has no plans to return to Mendocino. "I am done with the game," he says.

People like Sasso, Tom, and Ringo first moved to these remote ranches because they were perfect, secluded places to grow marijuana outdoors. But when CAMP raids pushed growers to begin growing indoors, they turned out to be far from perfect places to grow. Diesel spills in environmentally sensitive areas, especially along creeks and streams, have been a growing problem in Humboldt and Mendocino. Long-time residents complain about newcomers cutting down trees and leveling the landscape to put up massive grow rooms and causing erosion that clogs streams. Far larger numbers of people are growing indoors in houses in cities and towns all over the state, which has sometimes led to fires resulting from poorly wired lighting setups. Indoor grows are also susceptible to infestations of pests, mold, fungus, and other problems that can lead growers to douse their crops with chemical fungicides and pesticides. Given the legal gray zone around growing today and the possibility of making good money on indoor crops, more and more people are starting to grow this way. Indoor growing is so prevalent in the state that a 2011 independent report by Evan Mills, a staff scientist at Lawrence Berkeley National Laboratory, estimated that 3 percent of California's energy use goes towards indoor cultivation of marijuana.

Despite the very real environmental issues, electricity bills, and carbon footprint, these technologies have democratized the practice of growing, allowing anyone to grow whenever, wherever they please in a way that is very hard to detect.

One afternoon Marco takes me to visit a friend of his who lives down at the southern tip of San Francisco. He bought a house here on a dead end street with few neighbors. The owner has created a maze of grow rooms beneath the home where he lives. Walking through the cramped rooms in the basement of his home, he shows me a smaller version of many of the sophisticated systems that Marco uses. Many of the functions here are automated. His is not a huge operation—three grow rooms with about six lights each, one room for mothers, clones, and vegetative growth and two rooms for flowering. The owner says that he harvests about 6 pounds per room of Grand Daddy Purple every two months or so. He brings in a total of about 30 pounds of dried, cured marijuana a year that he sells to dispensaries for about $3000 a pound depending on the market. If all goes well he can earn about $90,000 a year before expenses from his basement operation.

Standing outside of his home, one that has a huge, open living space with stunning views of the water and a small back garden, a home that looks like thousands of others put up all over the Bay Area during the housing boom, I realize that it is nearly impossible to have any idea who is and who isn't growing marijuana.

Each house on this street, in the neighborhood, or city could easily have a small grow, something to help with the bills, with the retirement or vacation fund. Cannabis, which for thousands of years has grown wild and has been cultivated outdoors, has been bent almost completely to our will, to the point where it can be grown beneath the floor boards of the home it helps to pay for. With indoor, all it takes is a small amount of space, some initiative, a certain level of comfort with risk, and an outlet.

6 THE POLITICS OF MARIJUANA

Cannabis has been controversial in this country from the start. Today it is the plant's illegal status in a country where half the people think it should be legal that stirs up debate. At the beginning of America's history, though, the problem was getting people to grow the plant.

In the early 1600s, the settlers in Jamestown preferred to grow tobacco, which was in demand and quite lucrative. However, England needed hemp for rigging on its war ships. It was so hard to convince settlers to grow hemp that in 1607 they were required to grow hemp as part of their contract with the Virginia Company, according to Martin Booth's book *Cannabis, a History*. King James I made its production mandatory in the colonies in 1611. Booth points out that it took 80 tons of hemp to rig a Tudor man-of-war at a time when an acre produced just 18 pounds of fiber. Hemp fiber was also used to make paper and canvas for sails and clothes. Its seeds were pressed for oil.

In the 19th century, cannabis was a commonly used medicine often sold in tinctures in pharmacies. In Kentucky, Missouri, Nebraska, California, and many other states hemp was a cash crop into the early years of the 20th century. Through the 1920s the use of marijuana as a drug was rising and marijuana sometimes even found a place in popular culture: Louis Armstrong recorded an instrumental song called "Muggles," a slang for marijuana, in 1929 and Cab Calloway released a well-known song called "That Funny Reefer Man" in 1932. At the same time the press was increasingly linking the drug with crime and with Mexican immigrants. State legislatures, often driven by anti-Mexican rhetoric, began outlawing the drug one by one, beginning with California, soon followed by Texas, Iowa, Nevada, Oregon, and Washington. Ironically, many of these states would be on the forefront of legalizing medical marijuana by the end of the century. By 1931 there was so much concern over the effects of marijuana that cannabis was outlawed in 29 states. In 1933, one case drew a lot of attention from the press. On October 17 of that year in Tampa, Florida, Victor Licata woke in the middle of the night and, using an axe, killed both of his parents, his sister, and his two brothers. The police investigation discovered that Licata had used marijuana in the previous months; this revelation set off a wave of fear about the drug and its link to madness and violence. However, there was no indication that he was actually high when he committed the crimes. And, much more relevant, according to Booth, Licata had a documented history of mental illness and serious mental illness ran in his family. Despite the easy and salacious link between crime and drug use, it's far more likely that this tragedy was simply the act of a mentally ill young man.

This story was one of many that Harry J. Anslinger used to help outlaw marijuana nationally. Anslinger had been appointed to run the Federal Bureau of Narcotics at its inception in 1930. Though marijuana was illegal in many states, it had yet to be outlawed by the federal government. Anslinger highlighted stories like Licata's in articles that he wrote for various publications and whenever he spoke to the press. He used Licata's story when he testified before Congress in support of the Marihuana Tax Act (the act uses this spelling of the word), a law designed to tax the plant out of existence. Anslinger's views were opposed by only one witness, William C. Woodward, a representative of the American Medical Association, who testified about the plant's medicinal value. The bill became law in 1937.

The act required anyone growing, selling, buying, prescribing, importing, or giving away marijuana to register with the IRS and pay a series of fees from a $24 registration fee ($360 in today's dollars) to a tax of as much as $100 an ounce ($1500 in today's dollars). That absurdly high tax effectively outlawed the use of marijuana as a drug, and put an end to the centuries-old hemp industry in this country. Other countries began outlawing cannabis even earlier (the United Kingdom, for example, outlawed it in 1928) and with the implementation of the 1961 Single Convention on Narcotic Drugs, a treaty that has been signed onto by 180 countries, cannabis is now illegal in nearly the entire world.

Anslinger ran the Federal Bureau of Narcotics until 1962, a 32-year reign that would enable him to do more to shape our collective thinking about the plant than anyone else. Anslinger was incredibly savvy at using the media and popular culture to get his message across. He claimed that marijuana was more dangerous than cocaine or heroin, that it was linked to mental illness, depravity, and crime. Anslinger co-authored several books on the depravity caused by marijuana and the noble narcotics agents who risked their lives to bring in the bad guys. He and a co-author put together a pulpy account of drug culture called *The*

Murderers: The Shocking Story of the Narcotics Racket, its Rulers and its Victims, which was published in 1961 while he was still director of the agency. *The Protectors, Our Battle Against the Crime Gangs* featured a photograph of Anslinger with President Kennedy and a note praising Anslinger on his retirement in September of 1962. The book was published in 1964 after the president was assassinated. These books were filled with salacious tales of drug use of all sorts as well as the violence inherent in the organized crime groups that smuggled and distributed the drug.

In *The Murderers*, Anslinger relates one young person's description of a typical marijuana smoker's apartment:

> The room was crowded. There were fifty people but it seemed like five hundred. It was like crazy, couples lying all over the place, a woman was screaming out in the hall, two fellows were trying to make love to the same girl and this girl was screaming and crying and not making any sense. Her clothes were mostly pulled off and she was snickering and blubbering and trying to push these two guys away. . . . But I didn't want to do anything, I didn't want to sleep with those women or like that. I just wanted to lie down because the room seemed big and like a great tremendous crowd at a ball game or something.

Despite Anslinger's propaganda efforts, marijuana use continued to rise, reaching the counterculture in the 1960s and peaking in 1978 when 13.2 percent of the population over the age of 12 reported using marijuana in the previous month, about twice the percentage of users today. President Richard Nixon appointed a commission to review federal policy on the plant. The Shafer National Commission on Marijuana and Drug Abuse recommended relaxing the laws against cannabis use in 1972. Nixon ignored the report and went on to step up enforcement, declaring the War on Drugs that targeted marijuana as well as other drugs like cocaine, heroin, and later, crack, and that remains in effect to this day.

During Ronald Reagan's administration the drug war shifted from a rhetorical war to a more literal one with a boost in funding for enforcement, the appointment of a "drug czar," and anti-drug campaigns led by first lady Nancy Reagan. In 1981, 55,990 people were arrested for selling marijuana. By 1989 that number had grown to 84,425. In 1987 the Drug Enforcement Agency, the successor to Anslinger's Federal Bureau of Narcotics, seized nearly 1.4 million pounds of marijuana, a record that would not be broken until 2008, according to government records. Many growers and breeders moved to Holland to avoid getting caught. Others, under the relentless buzzing by law enforcement helicopters, took their growing indoors to avoid detection.

The War on Drugs did have an impact on public perception about the drug and even on drug use. According to the Monitoring the Future study at the University of Michigan, Ann Arbor, which conducts annual surveys of high school students, marijuana use among high school seniors fell during the 1980s and did not rebound again until the 1990s. According to an annual Gallup poll, support for legalization of marijuana nationally grew from 12 percent in 1970 to 28 percent near the end of the decade. In California support was even higher—a ballot initiative to legalize marijuana in California in 1972 received 33 percent of the vote—indicating more support than in the rest of the country but not close to a majority. It would be decades before attitudes would change significantly again. Support for legalization nationally lingered around 25 percent through the 1980s and 1990s and did not begin to rise notably again until 2000.

The other, perhaps unintended, consequence of the policy was to drive prices for marijuana up. As more people were arrested and supply decreased, the product became more valuable. And, of course, as prices rose, the lure of growing only increased.

In 1970 The National Organization for the Reform of Marijuana Laws, or NORML, was founded in Washington, DC, with the goal of repealing marijuana prohibition. Activists also began pushing for medical exemptions to the law, allowing sick people who found the plant effective for their symptoms to use it legally as a medicine. Some of the few studies conducted on smoked marijuana show that it can be useful for treating a range of conditions including helping those undergoing chemotherapy and those with AIDS to combat their nausea so they can eat. Over the years one activist after another went to jail for distributing marijuana to sick people to make the point that this was medicine. In 1991 Dennis Peron, a San Francisco medical marijuana activist, organized support for Proposition P, a resolution indicating the city's support for a statewide medical marijuana law. A year later he and others opened the state's first medical marijuana dispensary, the Cannabis Buyers Club, in the city's Castro district, in part to provide marijuana to those suffering from AIDS. The club was raided by state drug enforcement officers and the attorney general tried to shut it down.

In March of 1995 there was a meeting among some of the larger political groups in the legalization movement. Representatives from NORML and the Lindesmith Center, which was funded by billionaire George Soros who has a long history of supporting progressive causes (the organization would later become the Drug Policy Alliance, one of the most effective political organizations on this issue), attended. Other financial backers of the cause were there as was political consultant Bill Zimmerman, who works on progressive causes.

Zimmerman cautioned the group about the challenges of running a ballot initiative in California. Based on his experience, he told them that organizers would need to spend millions on advertising in order to conduct an effective campaign. They would need an extensive voter education campaign. Only when voters understood the issue, he cautioned, should the groups go ahead with a statewide initiative. Zimmerman conducted a survey and to his surprise found that one-third of the people contacted knew someone who had used marijuana for a medical reason—far more than he suspected. And that changed his thinking on the initiative. "I thought we had a good chance to win this," he says.

Despite Peron's long history of fighting for medial marijuana, he was not invited to the meeting with the activists and fundraisers. Like many on the ground in California, he was outside of the cadre of these well-funded East Coast organizations. Peron had his own plan. He and others drafted an initiative and collected 200,000 of the more than 430,000 signatures required to get the initiative on the ballot. At this stage, Zimmerman says, the other organizations and fundraisers including Peter Lewis, the chairman of Progressive Insurance, got involved and took over the signature-gathering drive. Lewis, who also supports progressive causes, would go on to fund the Marijuana Policy Project, another effective political advocacy organization. Once the medical exemption initiative, known as Proposition 215, was on the ballot, the organizations that had been surprised by Peron's initiative scrambled to help pass it.

Though polls showed that more than 60 percent of Californians supported the initiative, it was opposed by every elected official and law enforcement organization in the state. And the divisions between Peron and the advocacy groups continued to simmer. "Peron thought that he could win this by saying things like 'all marijuana use is medical,' and allowing himself to be photographed smoking a joint in his buyers club," says Zimmerman. "While we are trying to project an image of legitimate medicine, he is out there basically trying to legalize marijuana."

Nonetheless, the initiative passed with 55.6 percent of the vote. The next day the groups that backed it announced that they would begin drafting initiatives for other states. In 1998 voters in the states of Alaska, Washington, and Oregon passed medical marijuana initiatives. Maine and Nevada followed in 2000. In all, 15 states and Washington, DC, approved medical marijuana laws between the time California passed its initiative in 1996 and 2011, some through ballot initiatives and a handful through votes in state legislatures.

It has been a remarkable success for an issue that just a generation earlier would have been a non-starter. Framing marijuana use as a medical issue changed the debate. "The issue is about compassion for sick and dying people," says Steven Gutwillig, the California director of the Drug Policy Alliance, the group that has been behind many of the successful campaigns for medical marijuana. Instead of advocating for the rights of people to smoke marijuana, he says these laws focused on creating exemptions to the law that would allow sick people access to medicine. "This is about carving out an exemption to help alleviate the suffering of people," he says. "This group of people should not be persecuted for needing marijuana to relieve their suffering and that is a very strong message."

The fact that so many states have been allowing patients to obtain marijuana for over a decade has only helped the movement grow and has helped build support for legalization, says Gutwillig. In these states hundreds of thousands of people have been buying marijuana legally and, Gutwillig says, the chaos that opponents of the laws predicted—spikes in teenage drug use, increased crime, and auto accidents—have not come to pass. "The sky is not falling and that is showing that marijuana can be handled through a regulatory system," says Gutwillig. "That provides an illustration of what an alternative to prohibition might look like." And that experience has played out in the polling. According to an annual national poll conducted by Gallup, 31 percent of Americans supported legalization in 2000. In 2011, 50 percent approved it. There are few issues that have seen their support grow in a similar way. For example, support for physician-assisted suicide, though a very different issue, one that is sometimes decided at the polls, has barely changed over that same period, actually falling by a few points according to Gallup.

California's law is very different than those passed in other states. In every other state the laws were, for the most part, drafted with input from the Drug Policy Alliance and its allies or the Marijuana Policy Project. These groups put together model legislation that creates a state-regulated system. In Delaware, Rhode Island, and other states, dispensaries are licensed by the state. In Alaska, Nevada, Hawaii, and elsewhere, patients receive medical marijuana cards from a state-run registry. In Colorado, dispensaries are required to grow 70 percent of their own marijuana. Other states, including New Mexico, New Jersey, and Washington, DC, outlaw patient growing entirely, requiring dispensaries to grow all of their own marijuana, whereas Vermont, Oregon, Washington, and others allow patient cultivation. Laws in Arizona, Montana, Michigan, and Maine recognize patients with recommendations from other states. Maryland simply allows those using marijuana as a medicine to use that as a defense at trial if they are arrested.

The law in California was drafted by Peron and other activists; as a result, it is incredibly open-ended. It did not set up any of this statewide infrastructure. Instead it removed penalties for marijuana use, possession, or cultivation for those who have a physician's recommendation for marijuana to treat any one of a dozen or so diseases and a broad category of "other" symptoms. A subsequent bill passed in the state senate and signed into law in 2003, and later legal decisions, set a floor for the amount of marijuana that patients could possess—six mature and twelve immature plans and eight ounces of dried marijuana. Counties or cities could choose to allow more than that but no less. Local law could not override a physician's recommendation, so even if local law set a limit of 12 plants, with a doctor's recommendation for more, say up to 99 plants, a patient or his or her caregiver could grow 99 plants. Under the law, operators of dispensaries and cooperatives that follow the law are protected from state criminal sanctions.

Regulation of the system has been left up to cities and counties. As a result, everywhere is different. Arcata, in Humboldt County, requires its dispensaries to grow their own marijuana. A 10-minute drive away in Eureka, dispensaries can buy their marijuana from members. In Sacramento, the state's capital, it is legal to operate a dispensary in the city, but it is illegal to operate one in any of the unincorporated portions of the county. More than 200 cities and 24 of the state's 58 counties have bans on medical marijuana dispensaries. "We wish that there were a statewide system of licensing dispensaries," says Gutwillig. "It's a very loosey-goosey open-ended law."

What has resulted in California is a gray market where dispensaries are sometimes tolerated and sometimes not and patients are usually left alone. But few places have any policy about cultivation. Mendocino County has led the way on this issue. Anyone with a recommendation from a doctor in Mendocino County can grow up to 25 plants as long as they comply with some basic rules. For instance, they can't grow near a park, a school, or playground; a grow site must be more than 100 feet from another residence, behind a six-foot-tall, locked fence. Those seeking to grow between 25 and 99 plants have to register with the Sheriff's office. They need to pay a $1500 application fee, buy tags for each of their plants at $50 a piece, and pay a $500 a month inspection fee. According to Mendocino County Sheriff, Tom Allman, if registered growers exceed their limits, deputies will simply cut down the extra plants.

Allman began this program in 2007 as a voluntary one, initially giving tags away for free. When he wanted to start charging, the County Board of Supervisors was skeptical that it would work. "They told me I was the village idiot," Allman says. But they were wrong. By 2011 nearly 100 cooperatives had signed with his department and that has brought in over $600,000 in revenue over the years. The program has been effective, he says. "Fifteen years ago, a large marijuana grow was 2000 plants," Allman tells me. "Now a large grow is 300 plants." Allman tells skeptical police officers in other jurisdictions that by sanctioning grows under very specific conditions he has the benefit of knowing who is growing small amounts under the law. That frees him up to go after others who grow large amounts of marijuana illegally. And thanks to the revenue from his program, he now has the budget to do so.

But the program has not been embraced by everyone. No one knows for sure how many marijuana growers there are in Mendocino County, but it's a safe bet that it is far more than the 100 who have registered with Allman. Complying with the registration fees and regulations is expensive. Some growers are unhappy about having to provide law enforcement officials access to their property for inspections, what long-time activist Pebbles Trippet says is a surrender of constitutional rights. Some say that the program favors the larger growers who can afford the fees. And, of course, it does nothing to shield growers from the federal government. In October of 2011, the DEA raided Northstone Organics, a cooperative that was an early supporter of Allman's system that delivers marijuana to patients in the Bay Area. While agents cut down the plants and confiscated some equipment, they did not arrest anyone.

Mendocino is one of the few places in the state that has tried to address cannabis cultivation with a consistent policy rather than turning a blind eye and allowing the police to handle things as they see fit. From the perspective of many here it is a far cry better than ordinances attempted in Oakland and Berkeley that would have licensed massive, 50,000- and 30,000-square-foot indoor grow facilities in those cities, indoor farms that would be fierce competition for these growers. Those proposals were so audacious that the Department of Justice threatened to crack down on those facilities and government officials that approved them and the cities backed away from their plans.

Joey Burger, a second-generation marijuana grower from Humboldt County, wants to see a system like Allman's in place in Humboldt. Burger, who moved here with his parents when he was 14 years old, has been around marijuana since then and like many who grew up here says that growing marijuana was the only way to make a good living without leaving the area. College, he says, could actually set you back. "If you were lucky you graduated from high school and got to work for your parents or your brother," Burger says. "If you went to college, well, most of those kids came back here four years later to look for trimming jobs." By that time the ones who skipped college had already bought their own property and were growing for themselves.

Burger started the Humboldt Growers Association, a trade association for local growers. The goal was to create an organization that could give growers a say in how the county drafted its rules. He wants to pass laws that help to preserve the county's vast community of small-scale marijuana farmers. Burger favors doing away with rules that require dispensaries to grow their own marijuana since that cuts farmers out of the medical market. He also wants to tinker with the approach that Mendocino took. He says limiting the number of plants one can cultivate has pushed farmers to grow high-yield strains so they can make the most money from their allotted number of plants. In the process, quality can suffer, as can the region's competitiveness since some of the most desirable strains are relatively low yielding. Instead, he wants to see an ordinance that limits growing by the square foot. Burger says that outdoor growers should be able to have 100 square feet of canopy for each patient they grow for. And they should be able to grow for up to 200 patients. At the maximum, each grower here would be able to grow as many plants as they choose on nearly a half-acre. In Mendocino the 99-plant limit is per parcel of land. A grower in Mendocino who owns 10 parcels of land could grow 990 plants as long as there are enough members of the cooperative with the proper recommendations. Burger fears the potential for such large-scale growing. He wants the half-acre limit applied to the grower. "We don't want the big dispensaries from around the state coming up here, buying up land and blowing it up, taking away jobs from farmers," he says. His proposal would also impose significant local taxes, perhaps as much as $40,000 a year, for a half an acre.

Burger is one of the first to step out of the shadows and begin speaking openly about marijuana cultivation, something that more people are starting to do. As local governments here begin to address some of these issues, growers have found that they need to speak out and be heard or else they risk becoming the victim of laws that curb their ability to grow or make it impossible to provide marijuana to dispensaries. It has been a strange process. Many rural growers are independent, self-sufficient people who are used to keeping to themselves. They chose to break the law for a living and are therefore not particularly enamored of rules and law enforcement. But Burger's proposal has some others organizing and speaking up.

Charley Custer, who formed a separate group called the Humboldt Medical Marijuana Advisory Panel, says that Burger's proposal leaves the door open for large-scale grows that can be environmentally damaging, especially when newcomers show up, and cut down trees and level hilltops to grow. "A lot of people are in this just for the money," says Custer. "They are not part of the community and they do not contribute anything." Custer would like to see much better land-use planning around marijuana cultivation—and much smaller-scale growing. Here, as in Mendocino, the idea of paying fees to grow marijuana riles up many, who for years have been growing underground and augmenting the budgets of local government by contributing what they see fit through cash donations to road maintenance, schools, the fire department, and other government functions and doing just fine without having to wedge themselves into a regulatory system.

Regardless of how these counties regulate cultivation, it is in many ways remarkable that this public discussion is happening at all. Marijuana growers are hardly used to showing up at public meetings and airing their points of view on cultivation for the record. "The old-time growers are just panicked that we are talking about this," says the southern Humboldt grower Ty who has spoken out about how the country should address this issue as well as advocating for taxes on indoor growers that would discourage that form of cultivation. "They are like, 'Oh my God. You guys are going to get us all narced out.' It's kind of funny. They are imagining that the cops don't know that pot is being grown here—this part of southern Humboldt is infamous. And since we started speaking out about this, we haven't had a bust here."

Growers are finding that they not only have a voice but, as the real economic engine in this region, they may be able to actually shape the future for themselves, at least locally. Burger's group, for example, has hired a well-known Sacramento lobbyist to push his approach in Humboldt and in 2010 raised money for a candidate for city council who lost and for the district attorney's reelection campaign. While Burger is learning the ropes of local politics, marijuana money is already having a large impact on state politics—one that many growers here have not been happy with.

In 2010 an initiative to legalize marijuana in California was put on the ballot by an Oakland cannabis entrepreneur named Richard Lee. He was not well known by the policy groups in New York and Washington, DC, and his ballot initiative seemed to take them by surprise much as Peron's initiative had 14 years before.

Lee came to California in 1997 from Houston, Texas, where he owned a store specializing in hemp-based products, such as clothes, oils, and soaps. When Lee moved to Oakland he began working with Jeff Jones, another early medical marijuana activist, who had opened a dispensary near Oakland City Hall. Lee and Jones were among those who would push to make Oakland friendly to the medical marijuana industry. Like Wernard Bruining, who wanted to turn Amsterdam into the Jamaica of Europe, Lee wanted to turn Oakland into the Amsterdam of America. And in a way, he has.

He opened his dispensary, The Bull Dog, in 1999. He started Oaksterdam University in 2007, where students can learn how grow marijuana, how to set up dispensaries and collectives and navigate California's murky laws. The school occupies a 30,000-square-foot building in downtown Oakland. Under the Oaksterdam umbrella, he also has a gift shop, a head shop, a nursery that sells clones and mother plants, a glassblowing shop where bowls, bongs, and other paraphernalia are made, and even a cannabis museum. A medical marijuana patient gives people rides around nearby Lake Merritt in a Model T Ford emblazoned with the Oaksterdam logo.

Lee is a taciturn character. He wears sunglasses and when he talks, has a tendency to look down at his hands and fidget with the Velcro straps on the gloves he wears to avoid blisters from pushing the wheels of his wheelchair. Often his voice just trails off when he answers questions. Despite his inward nature, Lee has been incredibly successful here. He's treated a bit like the mayor of downtown Oakland. When he wheels himself down the street, people wave and say hello. Many come up and introduce themselves, others stop to talk shop about grow lights and ventilation systems.

He has also used the money he makes here to jumpstart the statewide and even national debate on the legalization of marijuana. In March of 2009 Lee paid for a poll that for the first time showed a majority of Californians supported legalization. The results were confirmed a month later by a Field Poll that found that 56 percent of California voters supported legalization. With the economic downturn and the ongoing budget crisis in Sacramento, Lee thought the argument for tax revenue that could come from the legal sale of marijuana would help bolster support. So, he spent over a million dollars of his own money to gather the signatures required to put a legalization initiative on the California ballot.

When the national advocacy groups got wind of his plans they asked Lee to hold off. 2010 was a midterm election. Young voters turn out in smaller numbers at the midterm and older, more conservative voters make up a larger portion of those casting ballots. "It was a terrible mistake to put that on the ballot in 2010 and we tried to convince him to, at a minimum, wait until 2012," says Zimmerman. Even Steve DeAngelo, the founder of the Oakland dispensary, Harborside Health Center, and a lifetime marijuana legalization activist, opposed putting the initiative on the ballot. "I didn't think it would win," he says.

Lee wasn't particularly interested in their analysis. "The guys back in New York, it's very arrogant for them to be like 'we know what's best.' They have no idea what is going on," says Lee. "It's just disappointing. But these people are very much removed from the battle scene. They are not out here taking the risks that we take every day. It's our decision to make, not theirs."

But Lee, like Peron before him, did need their help. He really only had the funding to get the initiative on the ballot, not the millions needed for a successful statewide campaign. And Lee's only initiative experience was running a successful ballot measure in Oakland, a far cry from guiding a controversial issue like this to victory. He needed funding and help from those with experience winning ballot initiatives. Just as these national groups came to the aid of Peron, they also came Lee's rescue. "Once it went on the ballot, I campaigned for it," says DeAngelo. "I urged everybody to vote for it. I voted for it."

But many Humboldt and Mendocino growers were unhappy with the initiative. They worried that it would give indoor marijuana growers in urban areas a competitive advantage. Their view was that the legislation was conceived by Lee, who has a lot to gain by bolstering his own businesses, which at least in part involve teaching new growers how to grow indoor marijuana for the urban market. Those rural growers were worried this bill would push them out of very the business they had created.

Lee did not help himself when he was quoted in a Humboldt County alternative weekly newspaper, the *North Coast Journal*, just four months before the election, trashing the outdoor marijuana grown there. He told the paper: "The outdoor, I was thinking they'll have to start making a lot of hash out of that," he said. "Bring a hash resurgence to the country. We haven't seen hash in the United States to any degree since the '70s, since it was coming into the country from Lebanon. Midnight Express. That holds a lot of history, right there."

Growers in Humboldt and Mendocino were outraged. They take great pride in the quality of their marijuana. To say that it should be used for hash is like telling a farmer specializing in heirloom tomatoes that his crop would make great juice. Most growers I spoke with brought this up whenever Richard Lee's name was mentioned. They felt that he had no respect for their historic role in the industry and no interest in seeing them succeed. Many growers also feared that prices would only fall further as the risk diminished and the industry would gravitate towards an agribusiness model if marijuana became legal. Large companies would move in and push them out just as small farmers were marginalized in legal agriculture. They did not want to be left out in the cold, their communities stripped of their only viable industry.

Even now with the election long over, when I ask Lee about the place that the north coast's outdoor growers might have in a legal industry, he doesn't do much to dispel their concerns. "How much could be moved to the Central Valley and put in greenhouses and done like cut flowers?" he asks. "There is some processing to it so it is a little special. A lot of it comes down to how it's legalized and if the government can try to put in restrictions to keep big agriculture out and make it more of a mom and pop thing. I don't know." Lee's statement is odd since Lee has been a key figure in actually writing that legislation and is likely to continue to be involved in the effort. If anyone would know, it's him.

Lee's legalization initiative, Proposition 19, lost at the polls in 2010 with 46.5 percent of the vote. It failed by a similar margin in Humboldt and Mendocino counties. Ty voted against it as did many growers. "The more legal it is, the harder it is for small farmers," Ty tells me. He's worried that with less risk, more people and larger companies will grow, driving prices down and making it harder for small outdoor growers to access urban markets, something they are already having trouble doing. "I voted partially out of my own greed, but I was really concerned that it was written by Richard Lee hoping to corner the market," says Ty.

Despite the loss and the acrimony in the growing community, most of the political advisors now agree that Lee was right to push the initiative forward. "It was a spectacularly successful investment," says Ethan Nadelmann, director of the Drug Policy Alliance, who initially opposed Lee's decision to put the proposition on the 2010 ballot. "It transformed and legitimized the debate nationally, even internationally. You have the *Wall Street Journal*, *The New York Times*, *USA Today* putting this on the front page of the newspaper with serious articles. That kind of national dialogue is transformational."

Lee, for his part, loves to see the big organizations admit that they were wrong, and that he was right. "Everybody agrees it was a very successful defeat. We have new allies, the labor unions, the civil rights organizations, presidents of other countries, the media coverage," says Lee. Vicente Fox, the former president of Mexico, supported Proposition 19 and the Global Commission on Drug Policy, a group that includes the former presidents of Mexico, Brazil, Colombia, the former secretary general of the United Nations and former secretary of State, George Schultz, has recommended that countries experiment with regulating cannabis in much the way that Lee's proposition would have. "It has been very nice to have all of these people call me up and say that they were wrong."

DeAngelo, however, does not think that he was wrong. "I was disappointed that it lost but I was not surprised," he says. His biggest worry is that the loss at the ballot box will indicate to the federal government that medical marijuana lacks support in the state. "Losses have consequences," he says. Just months after he told me that, in late 2011, the Department of Justice sent out over 100 letters threatening to seize the property of landlords that rent to dispensaries, admonishing media companies that sell ads to dispensaries, and raiding growers like Northstone Organics. Several dispensaries went out of business as a result and DeAngelo is mired in a fight with the Internal Revenue Service that contends that as a drug trafficking organization, his company cannot write off any expenses and owes $2.5 million in back taxes. IRS and DEA agents raided Lee's Oaksterdam University and Lee has since given up his role in the organization, though he plans to remain politically active.

Rather than push for all-out legalization, DeAngelo argues that advocates should continue to couch marijuana in the language of medicine and healing. "When you say legalization you are essentially going to the soccer moms of America and saying we should change the law because your kid needs one more thing to get high off of," he says. "That is not a wining argument." Instead, he wants to see laws that allow adults to purchase cannabis without a doctor's recommendation for broad purposes of wellness—anything from a serious medical condition like cancer to someone who wants to spark their creativity or libido. The current medical system, he says, has created an industry of "pot docs" who dole out recommendations for $45 a piece. "It breeds disrespect for the law, it breeds all of this uncertainty and abuse. Let's just say adult Californians can make this decision on their own." Of course, DeAngelo would like them to make that decision in businesses much like his medical marijuana dispensary.

7 MEDICAL DISPENSARIES RESHAPE THE BUSINESS

Harborside Health Center is hard to find. There is no massive sign out front to indicate its location. It's tucked away in a complex of single-story professional buildings on a quiet street by Oakland's inner harbor. But once inside, there is little question about where you are. Here cannabis is treated like a rarified product, one that buyers eagerly line up for and spend their time examining. THC-encrusted buds are displayed next to cards that indicate the strain and levels of cannabinoids including THC and CBD as well as the price. But customers here can buy much more than simple marijuana buds. Inside the display cases there is also hash, a range of tinctures, even soap made with hemp seed oil. There is an entire menu of THC-laden food available for sale—brownies, cookies, and carrot cake, even THChai tea. Because these drugs are displayed with the kind of remarkable care and orderliness common in only the most expensive retail shops, its easy to forget that what's on display here is an illicit drug throughout most of the country.

"I wanted to create an environment that was worthy of the plant, where patients could feel like what they were doing was not illegal or shady or unrespectable or weird," Steve DeAngelo, Harborside's founder, tells me as we stand in front of the display case. "I didn't want them to feel like they had to be a punk rocker or Rastafarian or a skate punk to feel comfortable in a medical cannabis dispensary. I really wanted to create an environment where just about any American could walk in here and feel comfortable."

DeAngelo grew up in Washington, DC, and became a medical marijuana activist in the early 1970s. Later he became a nightclub manager, a record producer, and a concert promoter—all while continuing his activism. When California passed its medical marijuana law in 1996, DeAngelo came west. But he was quickly disillusioned by what he saw. Dispensaries were often run by well-meaning activists with no business skills or those who DeAngelo calls "thug operators," who just set up a storefront, sometimes operating behind a bullet-proof glass window just doling out as much marijuana as quickly as they could with no concern for patients' needs. DeAngelo wanted to do something different. "I wanted to put together a cannabis dispensary that brought together the highest ideals of activism and professionalism," he tells me. "Being both an entrepreneur and activist my whole life, and cannabis being my focus my whole life, it was kind of a natural for me."

It has worked out well. Many point to Harborside as a model for the industry. The clinic did $22 million in business in 2010 and it strives for professionalism. There are two security guards in the parking lot who check that everyone entering has a valid medical marijuana card. The building has 23 security cameras and a staff person monitors the video feed at all times. New members are given an extensive orientation to the dispensary. A staff member verifies their medical recommendation, checking with the California Medical Board to make sure the physician is licensed. They must sign agreements indicating that they are joining the collective and authorizing other members of the collective to grow cannabis on their behalf. A staff member goes over the mission statement, the kinds of services available, explains the cannabis testing program, and gives new patients information on CBD-rich strains. There is no fee to join.

Harborside does not grow its own marijuana, as dispensaries in some cities are required to do. Instead it buys from its members, about 500 of whom are regular growers. Its standards are quite high.

Past a locked door that can only be opened with a fingerprint scan of a staff member is the room where growers bring their marijuana for consideration. DeAngelo tells me that Harborside rejects 90 percent of the marijuana that comes through the door. It may not be the strain they need at the time or just not high enough quality. It may have mold or some other problem. It could have problems with the cure resulting in buds that are too dry or too moist. It may not have been trimmed properly or it may have been harvested too early or too late, any of which can affect the appearance, smell, potency, or taste of the marijuana, making it less appealing to buyers. A light tube in the ceiling funnels a beam of natural light directly onto the counter where marijuana is examined (cannabis is best evaluated under natural light, DeAngelo says). His staff has magnifying glasses, microscopes, even a 200× electron microscope with which to examine the incoming product if they feel it is warranted. "Being at the epicenter of cannabis cultivation we can afford to be the most demanding, the most particular buyer that you'll find anywhere in the world," DeAngelo says. "We're kind of notorious in the grower community for being difficult."

For work such as this, DeAngelo has to hire people who know their way around marijuana. He has a human resources department that he says has a rigorous screening process that ensures that anyone hired has "a depth of knowledge about cannabis." This may be the only business in America where being a habitual pot smoker or having a past as an illegal grower makes one more qualified for a job.

Once the dispensary decides to purchase the marijuana, it is tagged with the date the bags were bought and the amount paid for it. The marijuana is assigned a batch number that stays with it even when it is broken down into eighths or grams so that if there is any problem (such as mold) it can be traced back to the source. DeAngelo says that he has virtually no problem with theft—less than 1 percent of the marijuana is lost each month, far below the loss rate for a normal retail business, he says.

Since California's law allows patients to grow for themselves and for their collectives, Harborside, like many dispensaries, does a large business in clones. These are also bought from outside growers. Harborside keeps clones on hand from about 40 to 60 different strains at any given time in trays in a room in the back under fluorescent tube lights. They are sold from a separate counter in the retail portion of the store. The most popular strains sell the best: OG Kush, anything in the Purp family, Sour Diesel and its offshoots. Jeremy Ramsay, who runs the clone program here, says that at peak season Harborside can sell up to 12,000 clones a week. When business is slow that can fall to 4000 a week—that's in the neighborhood of 400,000 plants a year from this dispensary alone.

At the end of each day all of the marijuana is locked up in a huge vault along with whatever cash is left over from the day's business. Harborside pays its growers in cash, so much of the cash that comes in from buyers goes out to growers. It also accepts credit cards. The vault is the only room in the dispensary without ventilation fans; in every other room, fans suck the air through charcoal scrubbers so the dense, heavy scent of marijuana is not vented into the neighborhood. Inside the vault, the air is thick with cannabis. Pound-sized bags of various strains of marijuana that have yet to be broken up into smaller denominations are stacked on metal shelves. "Oh my, Red Congolese," says DeAngelo stopping to open a bag and pull out a dense bud with a reddish hue. "Let me get some of that," he says as he puts the bud up to his nose and inhales. "We have so much good cannabis here," he says looking at the bags stacked up on the shelves. "I'm like a kid in a candy store."

Harborside is just one of many hundreds of dispensaries in California. Because California dispensaries are regulated by local government—sometimes county, sometimes city—there isn't a centralized list of dispensaries to be found anywhere. You'd have to check city-by-city to find out how many there are. Before Los Angeles cracked down at the end of 2009, estimates of the number of dispensaries there ranged from 545 to 800. However, after imposing a moratorium and attempting to rein the number in to 100 and even after one council member proposed banning them entirely, a 2011 estimate put the number of dispensaries at 500. Little had changed. Most cities have far fewer. San Francisco, with about 800,000 residents, has 35 dispensaries according to Weedmaps.com, a website where dispensaries can list themselves for free. This is hardly the most accurate source since many of those that close down may not remove their listing and many others may not choose to list themselves; it is, however, at least one centralized source. Oakland has half the population of San Francisco, but only a dozen dispensaries listed on the website.

Similarly, no one knows how many medical marijuana patients there are in the state. Since California does not require any sort of registration, only a doctor's recommendation, no agency keeps track. California NORML estimates that in 2010 there were between 750,000 and 1.2 million people that had medical marijuana recommendations in the state based on the percentage of the population that has received medical cards in Colorado and Montana, states that have state-run systems that track the number of patients. Between 2.5 and 3 percent of residents in those states are registered medical users. The one thing that is certain is that dispensaries like Harborside and its clientele are incredibly influential. They have had a hand in reshaping consumer expectations and appetites. Magazines, websites, blogs, and comments on message boards spread the word about the quality and diversity of marijuana here, which builds demand for certain strains and quality across the country. Growers and breeders are tailoring their approach to meet the desires of this increasingly educated and demanding market. Some growers here see the medical market as the market of first choice. What they cannot sell to dispensaries winds up on the illegal market, which has boosted the quality that buyers and hence suppliers expect in that market too. The legalization of marijuana for medical use in California has changed everything about the market for pot and is pushing changes for growers, breeders, and the plant itself.

Before dispensaries such as Harborside began displaying their buds in a jewelry-store-like atmosphere, giving buyers their choice of any one of several dozen highly popular, incredibly powerful strains to choose from, marijuana consumption in this country was different. Most Americans bought marijuana from a dealer (and the majority of Americans still do). Dealers rarely had more than one or two strains available depending on what they could buy from their connections. Sometimes a shipment of particularly good marijuana would come into town, sometimes not. No one knew the exact THC or CBD content. If you didn't like what that dealer, or two or three you might know, had on hand, you didn't smoke.

High Times magazine, which was launched in 1974, has presented their readers with exquisitely lit, detailed photos of huge marijuana buds for decades. The magazine essentially created its own genre of pot porn—it even has a pullout centerfold like *Playboy*. But outside of the educated consumers who spent their time flipping through its pages, few marijuana smokers had ever heard of the endless variations of Kush and Sour and Purp. Most people just smoked pot. Some of it was good and some of it wasn't.

One of the first named strains to take off in the Bay Area was Mendocino Purple because it was easy to identify and it was very high quality, says Kevin Jodrey. He's the cultivation director at the Arcata, California, medical marijuana dispensary Humboldt Patient Resource Center, and has been growing marijuana since the 1980s. "It was the first real, marketed, branded strain," he says. Since it was the only purple strain available at the time, the bud's mottled deep purple and green color became quick shorthand for quality. You could pull up in a car on a street in Oakland and the dealer could flash a bag of buds with a purple tint. As long as you saw the purple tint, says Jodrey, you knew you were getting top-quality marijuana.

With the advent of online message boards where smokers, growers, breeders, dealers, and everyone else with an interest in the plant gathers to hype up their strains and wax nostalgic about great buds, more and more smokers have been introduced to the incredibly varied world of the cannabis connoisseur. The more recent flood of interest in OG Kush was an Internet phenomenon, says Jodrey. "The Internet really hyped things up," he says. "All of a sudden people are thinking, 'Oh my God! I have to have that.'"

This shift followed the expansion of indoor growing, which was, in turn, driven by the government crackdown in the 1990s. Indoor marijuana is generally much more photogenic. It hasn't been battered around by the wind and rain, or subjected to airborne dust and dirt like outdoor marijuana. The buds of plants grown outdoors are often not as full and dense as those grown indoors, especially if they were not able to get full sun. Outdoor marijuana often lacks some of the visual qualities that buyers increasingly look for when they choose their marijuana. Indoor buds, grown in climate-controlled rooms, caressed by the constant subtle winds from fans, can be as visually perfect as any *High Times* centerfold. Some growers say they have a stronger taste and smell too.

Not long after indoor growing became the norm, the medical marijuana market started taking off in California and later, Colorado. Buyers became much more savvy. Walking into a dispensary is like walking into a well-curated wine shop. Just browsing is an education on the range of marijuana available and the care that is taken in the curing and trimming of high-quality cannabis. Perfectly presented buds of the popular strains that get the most time on message boards sell well and buyers get introduced to new powerful strains too. Today, with one batch of marijuana lined up against another in the dispensary display case, buyers are increasingly choosing what to buy based on how it looks. Buyers want to see dense buds showered with THC-laden crystals, a look that is a byproduct of indoor growing and much harder to achieve in marijuana grown outdoors.

In this environment marijuana grown outdoors is tough to sell, even for those who really want to sell it. DeAngelo, who laments the amount of electricity that is required for indoor growing, who philosophically aligns himself with the organic, outdoor growers, buys little outdoor marijuana because it simply does not sell very well. Despite their medical purpose, dispensaries are retailers and as retailers they have to stock what their customers want, otherwise those customers will move on.

Of course not all of California's dispensaries are massive urban retailers like Harborside. Most, in fact, are much smaller storefront operations often in small towns and cities up and down the state. One drizzly afternoon I meet Nathan Johns who runs just such a dispensary, the Hummingbird Healing Center, in Eureka, a town of 27,000 in northern Humboldt County. The dispensary is just across the street from a Subway sandwich shop in a long commercial building. Inside, two couches are pushed up against the wall with a coffee table in front of them as in a doctor's waiting room. But the rest of the room is full of stacked boxes. Johns is preparing to open up his dispensary again after it was shut down for a year because of a dispute with local government and a nearby dispensary over the kind of use permit he needs. So, today he is stocking up on marijuana.

Johns grew up in Sheboygan, Wisconsin, and after college had a job working in the accounting department at JPMorgan Chase in his home state. The work, he says, was uninspiring so he came out to California to work for the California Conservation

Corps building hiking trails in the Sierra Nevadas. Eventually he decided to move to Humboldt. He had been a marijuana smoker but never grew until he moved here. Soon he and a few partners decided to open the dispensary. "I'm a full-fledged medical marijuana rebel," Johns says, though with his wire-rimmed glasses and neatly combed hair he looks more accountant than rebel. "I love it, man. I really get a joy out of helping people."

With his reopening just a week or so away, he has scheduled meetings with several growers. That afternoon, while Johns is unpacking boxes, a grower who calls himself Jay Western Magic (who asked that he be identified only by this name) and his girl-friend Shannon arrive with a large black duffel bag stuffed full of one-pound bags of marijuana. Jay lives in a remote valley in Siskiyou County, far inland from here. He mostly grows indoors and has three grow rooms: two for production and one for breeding and experimenting. Jay, who has a thick mat of red hair and a goatee, is outspoken but has a gruff sort of kindness about him. Though he says that he'd like to grow more outdoors, Jay tells me that it's a bit like playing the lottery. This year he moved his plants and equipment to the site where he planned to grow and a bear came through and ruined everything. He came out again with all new plants and when he got those in the ground, chipmunks chewed through the wiring in the pumps and solar panels. After they repaired that damage and wrapped everything in wire mesh to ward off the chipmunks, another bear chewed the water line in half. "We're only two weeks in," says Jay. "This is going to be one of those years."

Jay, like other growers looking to sell their marijuana to dispensaries, spends part of his time leading the life of a traveling salesman. He drives from dispensary to dispensary with duffel bags full of marijuana hoping to sell as much as he can at every stop. It is not easy and many dispensaries only want to buy a small amount at a time of a wide range of strains.

While we sit, Johns opens the duffel and starts pulling out and examining Jay's one-pound bags of marijuana.

"This is Afghani from Afghanistan and we brought the seeds here. It was freaking huge," says Jay noting that the two areas are on a similar latitude with similar growing seasons, the reason that growers have planted indicas here for decades. "Fourteen feet tall and twelve feet across—buds the size of this table," he says, thumping his fist on the coffee table.

Johns, far more interested in what he is looking at in the plastic bags than in Jay's tales of towering plants, pulls another bag from the duffel. "What's this?" he asks.

"Outdoor Dynamite," says Jay. It's a strain that Jay says originated within the Asian community in British Columbia and was used by a healer. Jay says he uses it every day. Pointing to another bag he says, "That one is Purple Kush by Hashberry, mine, hydro, indoor." In English, that is a strain that's a cross between Purple Kush and Hashberry that Jay grew hydroponically, indoors. Jay has also brought along several pounds from other growers.

"And this?" Johns asks holding another bag.

"That is Diesel Dynamite. That was all I had right now. There's more that is hanging," says Jay. "It's not ready yet."

"Will I be able to get some in by the first week in July?" Johns asks.

"Yeah."

Johns holds up another bag, looks at it skeptically and asks, "Is this your stuff or someone else's?"

"That is hydro OG," says Jay. "It's from a buddy of mine."

"Can I sample it?" Johns asks, explaining that he already has some and may not want to buy more.

"Please do. I told him not to spend the money I gave him on that. I told him it was B grade," says Jay. "And he still wants too much money for B grade."

Johns buys everything from Jay except for the questionable OG.

That went much more smoothly for Jay than it does for most growers, in part because these two have worked together before and in part because Johns is starting up and needs to buy a lot of marijuana. Even selling to long-time contacts, making a living this way can be tough.

Jay spends a lot of time on the road, especially since he lives in such a remote area. The 180-mile drive here on narrow back roads took Jay and Shannon most of the day. He sells to two other dispensaries in Humboldt and others across the entire northern half of the state including three in Redding, one in Chico, and three in Sacramento. He knows that if he gets pulled over, he may well get arrested due to the erratic adherence to the state's medical marijuana law from county to county. He keeps his dispensary membership papers in order and never carries small baggies that might make police suspect that he is breaking up the marijuana to sell on his own. He calls the dispensaries he is visiting to let them know he is on the way and to be aware that if he does not show up when expected, he has probably been arrested. "That is the problem," Jay says. "The legitimacy of this business really needs to be there."

This routine is incredibly time consuming and can be a demoralizing experience when dispensary after dispensary either offers to pay very little or rejects the crop outright. Dispensaries are under no obligation to buy any marijuana from their member growers and often they reject far more than they buy. Though Johns bought most of what Jay had to offer, that is unusual.

Harborside, for example, rejects 90 percent of the marijuana that comes through the door. It is just another added layer of work and frustration for some growers.

Many outdoor growers have already given up on California's dispensary system. The back-to-the-land grower Sean says that dispensaries low-ball growers and they have little interest in outdoor marijuana. He has stopped trying to sell to dispensaries altogether. Tom from Spyrock Rd. laughs when I ask him if he ever sells to dispensaries. "What, are they going to buy a couple of pounds from me? They want to have a couple of pounds of this and a couple of pounds of that always on hand. I want to sell a hundred pounds. I want to sell five hundred pounds or something at a time," Tom says. "I want to be done with it. I don't want to run down to San Francisco every week to sell a couple of pounds." The dispensaries are much better set up to buy from indoor growers who produce smaller quantities of marijuana throughout the year instead of outdoor growers who harvest theirs all at once like Tom does. While the dispensary model as it is being played out here in California meets the dispensaries' needs quite well, it doesn't do much for a lot of growers, particularly those in Humboldt and Mendocino, who often feel left out of the system completely because they are far away from urban centers where most dispensaries operate and because the dispensaries are most interested in indoor crops. Most of these growers simply return to selling marijuana to the illegal market as they always have.

But that market too has changed. So many people are now growing marijuana in California that growers say prices on the black market have plummeted from as much as $5000 a pound at the peak in California in 1995 to as low as $1200 a pound in 2011 depending on the strain and the quality of the marijuana.

The wholesale price that growers get when they sell to those who ship the marijuana cross-country to be sold illegally has mirrored the price decline in the medical market. Both markets have faced a surplus of product and prices have plummeted as a result. And they may well fall further. As Sean told me, "In the past, dealers were looking for marijuana to buy. They always paid up front in full. It was a seller's market for decades." But, much like the housing market after the bubble burst, the marijuana market has been turned on its head. Growers must now spend time hunting down buyers who collect crops for underground distributors. Instead of getting paid upfront, growers must now give their crop to these buyers only to be paid when the marijuana is sold, often on the other side of the country. Sometimes the dealer doesn't like the product and returns it. Plenty of people get caught driving marijuana across the United States, and when that happens, no one gets paid. Sometimes just working with the wrong person can have consequences. Sean says that he once sent a crop out with someone who seemed "shaky" to him. "He ended up passing it along to someone else who didn't pay him and suddenly we are out," he says. "When you send the product out first and then get paid you are a lot more open to trouble." On the black market, it is now possible to never be paid for at least some of your crop.

With Colorado also supporting a significant medical marijuana market, growers from there are also flooding the east coast with high-quality marijuana, growers told me. And that is putting another dent in the need for California cannabis, which must travel further at greater cost and risk of arrest to get to east coast markets.

To top it all off, even with all of this risk and the plummeting prices, dealers are still incredibly picky. They only want the most desirable strains and, like the dispensaries, are quick to reject anything that was not grown, harvested, and cured very well. The medical market has raised the bar for quality, even in the illegal market. Consumers are much more picky and they are getting what they want—a far better product. Mediocre marijuana no longer sells well. Dealers are not beyond simply rejecting marijuana that does not meet their standards. It's a very different world compared to when Sean's father Paul started growing, when there was a nearly insatiable demand for crops here. "Today," Paul says, "to even sell it at all you have to have stuff that is primo."

The links between the illegal and the medical market are remarkably strong today. Trends, prices, demands, even supply in one influence the other. But that changes when it comes to providing medicine to those with devastating diseases. It turns out that what may be most helpful about cannabis as a medicine has almost no value at all as a recreational drug.

8 CANNABIS AS MEDICINE

Inside the Hummingbird Healing Center in Eureka, Jay Western Magic takes a small box filled with about two-dozen bottles out of his duffel bag. He removes one from the box and hands it to Nathan Johns, the director of the dispensary. The brown glass bottle, which has a lid with a dropper attached, looks like those that contain eardrops or infant's aspirin—except for the label, which features a red cross with a marijuana leaf superimposed over it.

This is Jay's glycerite. He cold presses the leaves of the Dynamite strain with glycerine, a thick, sweet, inactive liquid commonly used in herbal extractions. The resulting compound has no psychoactive effect because the delta-9-tetrahydrocannabinolic acid (THCA) in the plant is not psychoactive until it is heated. It is transformed to the psychoactive THC when heated to 222 degrees Fahrenheit or more by smoking or cooking. The glycerite has the rank smell of month-old bong water and tastes overwhelmingly sweet. Patients are instructed to place drops (anywhere from just a few drops to a dropper-full a day) under the tongue. Jay sells his glycerite at dispensaries across northern California. He even sells sweatshirts that advertise the product. The glycerite, he tells me, has saved lives. "People who have four months to live are now back to work. People who had full-ride disability are now playing golf," he tells me. "We get emails weekly of these stories. If I didn't get them myself, I wouldn't believe it."

Jay hands me a flier that he gives out along with the glycerite. It claims that the medicine provides relief for 22 different ailments including migraines, Parkinson's disease, bipolar disorder, spinal cord injuries, Huntington's disease, Alzheimer's disease, and cancer. Jay seems sincere. Like many growers that I've met, he feels passionately about the medical benefits of the plant and wants to provide medicine to heal the sick. Many Humboldt and Mendocino growers give away leaf, buds, or oil to sick people, earning nothing from it at all. They are happy to provide a service, to help those who are suffering and looking for relief. And there is enough anecdotal evidence floating around the Internet to suggest that cannabis provides relief for everything from hangnails to brain tumors to our most debilitating diseases. It is hard to believe that any single plant can ever address such a broad range of totally unrelated ailments. There is simply little or no published research to back up many of these claims. In fact, despite its long history of use as a medicine in the United States and elsewhere, smoked cannabis, let alone the oils, juice, and extracts sold in dispensaries here, remains poorly studied in this country.

A 2009 report by the American Medical Association's Council on Science and Public Health found that in the previous 35 years fewer than 20 randomized controlled trials had been

conducted on smoked cannabis and published in English language journals. Those studies had a total of about 300 participants. This paltry level of research is no accident, particularly
here in the United States.

Cannabis is classified as a Schedule I drug along with drugs
like heroin, MDMA (commonly referred to as ecstasy), and LSD.
Part of the definition of a Schedule I drug is that it has no medical benefit. The only source for marijuana for a medical study is
the University of Mississippi. Researchers hoping to obtain marijuana must be approved by the National Institute on Drug Abuse,
or NIDA, part of the Department of Health and Human Services,
which contracts with the university to grow marijuana. Those
seeking funding from NIDA for their study must pass through
three levels of review in order to be approved. But even those who
have their own funding, who are not seeking a dime from NIDA,
must be approved by a review panel at the heath and human services department before NIDA will grant access to its marijuana.
Then researchers must also prove they can comply with stringent
Drug Enforcement Agency security requirements.

Rick Doblin, the founder of the Multidisciplinary Association for Psychedelic Studies, which researches the medical benefits of drugs like LSD, MDMA, and cannabis, says that this
review process is unlike any for studies of other Schedule I drugs.
He has been involved with medical studies on the therapeutic
value of MDMA, for example, and has been able to obtain the
drug through one of several laboratories licensed by the government to make it without having to obtain approval from NIDA.
The only reason that researchers need to go through NIDA's
process is that NIDA is the only legal provider of marijuana in
the country. Doblin's organization is suing the agency over its
rejection of his FDA-approved study of the therapeutic value of

smoked cannabis on veterans with post-traumatic stress disorder or PTSD. Although the FDA approved the study, he says the health and human services panel evaluates research proposals from a basic science perspective, not a drug development perspective. He says that the panel, which primarily reviews grants, raises basic science questions about the mechanisms behind the proposed efficacy of cannabis that the FDA is unconcerned with. "In order to make a drug into a medicine, you don't need to know *how* it works, you just need to know *that* it works," says Doblin. The department approves far more studies of smoked cannabis that probe its negative effects—memory loss, addictiveness, impairment of motor skills—than those that study its potential medical benefits. "That they are blocking the PTSD study is outrageous," Doblin says. "Vets are committing suicide from PTSD and many report that marijuana is helpful yet NIDA and health and human services are blocking the research."

In addition, those who do get access to the marijuana are usually given cannabis that is unlike anything available through medical dispensaries today. The THC levels range from a placebo at 0 percent to a maximum of 8 percent, whereas the THC in marijuana that patients can buy at dispensaries is usually around 20 percent. The government facility does not grow a wide variety of strains and it does not categorize its plants by the strain names used in the illegal and medical markets. Researchers hoping to focus on the effects of cannabinoids other than THC are unlikely to find strains rich in CBD, for example, available through the government. Though other researchers have applied for permits to grow different strains for medical research, the government has denied all of those requests.

Despite this, many medical benefits of cannabinoids have been well documented and the basic mechanism by which cannabis affects users is well known. There are two kinds of receptors in the body—called CB1 and CB2 receptors—to which cannabinoids bind. CB1 receptors are found primarily in the central nervous system, mostly in areas of the brain responsible for movement, memory processing, and pain modulation, as well as other areas. The CB2 receptors are found in the immune system, the gastrointestinal systems, the peripheral nervous system, and to a lesser extent in the brain. Our bodies naturally produce their own endogenous cannabinoids or endocannabinoids that stimulate these receptors just like we produce endorphins (endogenous morphine). Cannabinoids introduced into the body from marijuana are called phytocannabinoids. These phytocannabinoid molecules are shaped just like the endocannabinoids our bodies produce naturally, and they stimulate the same receptors.

This endocannabinoid system plays a role in a vast range of functions and in the interaction between the body's various systems. How cannabinoids affect us is determined by which receptors are activated and where. Cells generate and release endocannabinoids as a result of certain signals. For example, if one neuron releases a certain level of electrical activity towards another neuron, the targeted neuron may respond by releasing endocannabinoids. These travel back to the excited neuron's CB receptors and slow it down. This can be valuable because overexcitement of brain cells can cause them to die and is a contributor to stroke and epilepsy. In this way Cannabinoids act as a neuroprotectorant. Endocannabinoids often act as modulators, regulating activity within different systems—activation of the CB2 receptors in the immune system, for example, will help slow swelling. Phytocannabinoids trigger the same reactions as those we produce naturally, which is why cannabis is known as an anti-inflammatory, for example. The scope of the endocannabinoid system is the reason that cannabis is being investigated for such a broad range of medical uses.

The research that has been conducted on smoked cannabis has found that it is an effective pain reliever, that it improves appetite and weight gain in patients with reduced muscle mass, and may relieve muscle tightness and pain in patients with multiple sclerosis, or MS. Surveys show that those with chronic pain, MS, and Lou Gehrig's disease use it to relieve some symptoms and people with HIV or hepatitis C smoke marijuana to relieve pain, nausea, appetite suppression, sleep disorders, and to counter the side effects of antiviral drugs. According to one review, between 2005 and 2009, 37 published studies examined the medical benefits of cannabis—smoked as well as in extracts like Sativex and synthetic THC—across a range of symptoms. These studies (eight of which were on Sativex) generally found that cannabinoids were effective pain relievers, helpful with muscle tightness and spasms of those with MS, helped with overactive bladder problems and incontinence, boosted caloric intake and weight gain in HIV patients, reduced intraocular pressure in glaucoma patients, and even found that CBD helped reduced acute psychosis in those suffering from schizophrenia even as THC had little or no effect. One study found that THC inhibited tumor cell proliferation in vitro.

The research is clear that THC and CBD have important medicinal properties. Research also suggests that other cannabinoids and terpenes may also have important uses as well. However, those who ingest these compounds by smoking cannabis are subject to some negative health effects. While high, smokers have an impairment of short-term memory and their motor skills and reaction times slow due to the reaction of the CB receptors that are flooded with phytocannabinoids in the parts of the brain that control those functions. They also have trouble understanding complex information. It has also caused anxiety, panic, and confusion in a minority of those studied. Regular cannabis smokers do develop increased symptoms of bronchitis, yet, perhaps counterintuitively, there is no evidence that links habitual cannabis smoking to lung cancer.

While the problems with cannabis use are well documented, the drug is far less dangerous and less addictive than many opiate derivative drugs currently approved for medical use. Fewer than 10 percent of regular marijuana smokers become dependent. And, with the goal of facilitating more research, even the AMA has called for the government to review the status of cannabis as a Schedule I drug.

In order to gain a comprehensive understanding of cannabis, an incredible amount of study would be required. The plant is remarkably complex. As many as 80 distinct cannabinoids have been isolated and there are over 120 terpenes that give the resin its odor and flavor. Individual cannabinoids have their own value in a traditional pharmaceutical approach where a useful molecule is isolated, synthesized, patented, and made into a pill. Marinol, which is synthetic THC, has been approved by the FDA to treat nausea and vomiting in patients undergoing chemotherapy and loss of appetite and weight loss in patients with AIDS. Patients who take Marinol do not have the respiratory effects associated with smoking marijuana and, according to the labeling required by the FDA, only about a quarter of those who take it report feeling high. Some studies, however, suggest that smoked cannabis with its range of cannabinoids and terpenes has a similar effect on nausea as Marinol. Other cannabinoids also show much promise. Cannabidiol (CBD) has been shown to relieve pain, control muscle spasms, curb anxiety, and to be a neuroprotectorant; it also shows some promise in fighting tumors. Cannabinol

(CBN) has been shown to have anti-convulsant and anti-inflammatory properties. Cannabigerol (CBG) has been demonstrated to relieve pain and may help to lower blood pressure and reduce anxiety. Terpenes have other effects. One of them, mycrene, has been shown to reduce inflammation. These are just a fraction of the cannabinoids and terpenes in the plant.

Dr. Geoffrey Guy, founder of GW Pharmaceuticals, says that the complex interactions between these elements naturally found in the cannabis plant add benefits that cannot be found in products that synthesize a single molecule. CBD, for example, is believed to counter the high brought on by THC so when the two are combined, users get the benefits of the cannabinoids with less of the high sensation. The company is studying about a dozen of the most promising cannabinoids and combinations of them to determine if they hold promise for new extracts like Sativex. But studying the interactions between all of these elements adds an incredible layer of complexity to any research. There is so much to know about this poorly studied plant that even without the legal barriers in this country, we'd likely still be poking around in the dark trying to learn what we can.

This incredible uncertainty puts patients in a terrible situation. Those living in the majority of states where cannabis is completely outlawed must buy it illegally if they choose to do so. If they live in a state with a medical marijuana system, they can get access to the plant, but they can never be sure exactly which of the myriad strains they can buy is going to be most effective. They have to muddle their way through by trial and error. When they do find a strain that works for their condition they will inevitably stick to that. But they have no way of knowing whether that is the most effective strain or simply one that has some impact. Is there a better way to get the effect they are looking for—eating rather than smoking, taking a pill or tincture, or even drinking juice? Some of these preparations are even less well studied than smoked cannabis. The best that patients can do is make decisions based on anecdotal evidence, which can be incredibly confusing and unreliable.

That's not to say that good dispensaries don't have a solid grasp of what we do know about the plant and how various strains and delivery mechanisms might affect the patients. Harborside employees ask customers what they are medicating for, what time of day they use the medicine, what other activities they'll be engaged in, whether or not they'll be in public, as well as their budget. The answers to these questions will drive not just what strains the clerk might recommend, but what form of delivery they choose as well. DeAngelo explains that someone who can't sleep because of chronic back pain should not smoke cannabis because it won't last as long as they need. Instead he recommends a capsule that will last six to eight hours. Someone with early morning nausea might have trouble keeping a capsule down and may not want to be high for eight hours at work. That person would want a sublingual spray that would wear off in 90 minutes or so—enough to help overcome their morning nausea while still allowing them to get through work with a clear head. "You have to have a staff that understands how to help patients through that kind of choice," DeAngelo says.

Even though some dispensaries have knowledgeable and well-trained staffs, it's certainly not a requirement. And overall the market remains poorly regulated. Cannabis has not been approved by the FDA to treat anything, so it is not regulated by that agency. Since it is illegal, the federal government can't regulate it as a supplement or herb. In California the state does not regulate it either—that is left up to local government. And no one seems to regulate the kinds of claims that growers like Jay Western Magic make about their products. As a result, there are plenty of wild assertions about the efficacy of various medicinal products. Some growers have started making oils from the plant that are used topically and are said to cure tumors. Others have begun juicing the leaves, something that they say has incredible health benefits and has no psychoactive effect since the cannabis has not been heated. But none of these unique approaches has been subjected to much, if any, scientific scrutiny.

The United States is hardly the only country grappling with how to let patients obtain medical marijuana. Canada has a system, as does Holland. While GW Pharmaceuticals is based in England and has a special license to grow marijuana there, the plant remains illegal in the United Kingdom. Israel's system may be one of the best. It is a nationwide, centralized system with controls that recognizes the need to regulate growers while allowing them to compete. Physician recommendations are reviewed and sometimes rejected, distribution is tightly controlled, and growers there are licensed by the government.

Following a court case in 1999, a small number of patients in Israel (only two patients in the year 2000) were able to obtain cannabis from the government. At that time, there were no government-sanctioned growers or dispensaries. The government simply gave these patients hash that had been confiscated from drug dealers. Eventually officials became concerned that patients might receive tainted medicine—no one knew where the confiscated hash was coming from or how it was made. That uncertainty caused officials to change course. At first they allowed patients to grow their own marijuana. But it can take the better part of a year to grow and harvest an outdoor plant. And many patients were not in good enough health to grow the plants themselves. So, the government allowed some patients to grow for others. Eventually, under pressure from activists, the government decided to create a centralized system under the Ministry of Health.

Today, patients suffering from chronic pain, HIV, Crohn's disease, MS, glaucoma, and a few other illnesses can get a recommendation from one of about a half dozen physicians in the country who are allowed to recommend marijuana. These physicians must be board certified in the area for which they are prescribing marijuana. Each recommendation must be reviewed by Dr. Yehuda Baruch, the program's director. He says that he rejects about 20 percent of the recommendations primarily because the regulations require that those receiving cannabis for pain have an organic source for their pain. Those who report pain with no physical source for it cannot obtain cannabis.

At the end of 2011, Israel's 9000 medical marijuana patients picked up their cannabis at one of five distribution points in the country, most of which are in hospitals. The health ministry is working on expanding the system to include distribution at pharmacies, which will help make cannabis more accessible as the number of patients rises. According to Doblin, who consulted with the government on designing the program, the biggest drawback is that there are so few doctors who can recommend marijuana—a little more than one doctor for every million Israelis. And each recommendation must be personally reviewed by a single person—Dr. Baruch.

Growers were among those instrumental in creating the system, which may be why Israel's approach actually takes them into account. Yohai Gild, a co-owner of Trichome Technologies along with Kenny, founded a company called Better to grow marijuana for the Israel's health ministry using growing technology and strains from Trichome. When Better started growing in Israel in 2007, it was required to give away all of its marijuana with the thought that some day it would be able to begin selling cannabis to patients legally. Gild and his competitors did just that, losing money for two and a half years. "All of my friends that I started out growing with for dispensaries in the US are millionaires now," Gild says with a laugh. In 2010, the Israeli government finally allowed these growers to start charging for their marijuana. The cost is remarkably low—about $2 a gram or $7 for an eighth of an ounce. That same amount of high-quality marijuana sells for about $50 at Harborside in Oakland. The government has imposed rigorous security requirements. Gild is required to have his grow facility ringed by a six-foot-deep underground wall that is topped by an electric fence. The facility must be equipped with security cameras. Any amount he ships over 1.75 ounces must be transported in an armored truck with four armed security guards and the marijuana itself must be in a safe with one-foot-thick walls. Yet, even with these security costs, he estimates that it only costs him about $0.50 a gram to grow the marijuana in greenhouses. With just a few thousand regular patients, the venture would be quite profitable.

Gild has also been breeding strains better adapted to the desert environment. And he has been working to find strains that have some level of CBD. One strain that Gild developed using Purple Kush, Sour Diesel, and a Bedouin strain has a THC level of 22 percent with about 1.2 percent CBD. It's called Better Kush. The government has been pushing growers to produce these CBD-rich strains. "We'd like to see more strains with more CBD," says Dr. Baruch. "We are very optimistic."

Here in the United States, even without any centralized system for marijuana production, CBD is starting to gain some attention and a few dedicated breeders are working on developing CBD-rich strains. Lawrence Ringo, who owns the Southern Humboldt Seed Collective, is one such breeder. On a drizzly late-spring morning I set out to meet him. I drive for several miles on increasingly narrow, twisting dirt roads, and then, after turning next to a wrecked car, I descend down a rocky, muddy drive past an old tarped-over school bus and several greenhouses. Past the chickens and the barking dogs the drive ends under a large live oak next to Ringo's two-story off-the-grid house. He tells me that on a clear day you can see all the way to the ocean.

Ringo and I walk up the hill towards one of his greenhouses. "This is what I call the boys' room," he says as we enter a greenhouse covered with translucent plastic sheeting. A chicken paces around the room as we talk. There are several three-foot-tall, male marijuana plants in the middle of the room. Ringo turns on the radio. The plants, he says, like the music. "I treat these plants like gods," he says. "And they give me the biggest, baddest pollen you've ever seen."

With so much focus on the medicinal uses of marijuana, Ringo and many other breeders are changing their approach. For decades breeding was done with the goal of creating high-yield, quick-flowering plants with ever-higher THC levels. "Over the years of doing this, I've been looking for the best, the gnarliest strains, something I can take a toke of and it knocks me on my ass," says Ringo. Now, he and a handful of others are starting to look for totally different qualities in their plants. They want strains that are low in THC and high in CBD—plants that won't knock anyone on their ass.

High CDB plants are so rare because THC and CBD compete with each other for a place in the plant. The two cannabinoids actually occupy the same spot on the chromosome. Two genes—the BT and BD genes—determine whether a plant produces THC, CBD, or both. Plants that inherit only BT genes from both parents will produce only THC and, conversely, those with only BD genes from both parents will produce only CBD; those that inherit one of each will produce some of each. And over time, recreational breeders have been selecting for those BT genes to create plants that produce the most THC. As a result, most commercial marijuana strains have lots of THC and miniscule amounts of CBD, if any at all.

In 2002, Ringo began trying to breed a strain of marijuana that would help him with his chronic back pain. He began with a Sour Diesel that he worked on stabilizing, crossing the females with Sour Diesel pollen that he had saved for several years in a row. Then a friend showed up with what he calls a "Purple Chunk thing called Ferrari." He crossed his stabilized Sour Diesel with that to make a strain that he named Tsunami. It had the taste of cream soda, Ringo says. When he smoked it, he says the plant had what he calls a body high, very pleasant but not mentally overwhelming. The next year, he decided he wanted it to taste more like Sour Diesel, so he crossed that plant with his Sour Diesel pollen. "It turned into something else completely," Ringo says. "It didn't taste anything like Sour Diesel. You smoke it and you can never get high on this shit, but you feel great, really centered." And, Ringo says, it did wonders for his back: "Now I can smoke a big fatty and not get high, but there is no back pain. It's pretty cool." He called it Sour Tsunami.

Later Ringo met Samantha Miller, a woman who had just opened a lab called Pure Analytics to do gas chromatography testing of marijuana for dispensaries and growers so they can determine the exact cannabinoid profile of their plants. Ringo decided to get his Sour Tsunami tested, hoping to learn why it was so different from his other plants. "She called me up freaking out," Ringo says with a laugh. His plant was producing over 11 percent CBD (he has since refined the strain, raising its CBD level to nearly 14 percent). That call from the lab was the first that he had ever heard of CBD.

Until 2008 there were no labs that tested marijuana in California. Growers and breeders simply had to use their judgment about a plant—how it grew, its taste, smell, and effect—to guide their breeding. That changed when Steep Hill Labs opened in 2008. Steve DeAngelo was one of the co-founders—he wanted to get a better sense of the cannabinoid levels in the marijuana that he was selling at Harborside. More than a half dozen labs have opened up since then, including the one Ringo uses. Now lab results indicating the levels of THC and CBD in the plant are displayed alongside buds in dispensaries more and more often—a homegrown kind of self-regulation that is increasingly popular with buyers and dispensaries. Without these labs, growers like Ringo would have no idea that they were sitting on important CBD-rich strains.

David Lampach, another co-founder of Steep Hill, says that the lab had been testing samples for months before one came in that had any CBD. In the beginning the compound surfaced in about one in a thousand or more samples. That is not surprising, given that CBD was essentially bred out of the plant here. Since CBD-rich plants are often low in THC, dispensaries rarely bought this marijuana and as a result rarely sent them out to be tested. Then, over time, a handful of strains started coming through the door that were high in CBD. The lab began working with an organization called Project CBD to contact the growers of these CBD-rich strains to educate them about the value of CBD. That is how a grower and breeder who goes by the name of Shadrock found out what he had developed.

Shadrock had never smoked marijuana before he suffered several herniated discs in college. He hated the painkillers he was prescribed for his back pain. Eventually, he tried marijuana. Cannabis dampened the pain enough so that he could be active again. While living in Massachusetts, he began to grow and breed marijuana to help with his pain. He had a mother plant of the Mountain Lion strain, a potent but lanky strain that was not great for indoor growing. He wanted to boost its yield so he tracked down a strain called Jamaican Yarder, a sativa that could grow up to 18 feet tall and was known for its very high yield. He crossed the two plants, was able to grow out the offspring, and began stabilizing the strain to produce some seeds of what he called the Jamaican Lion. Then in 2006, he had to pick up and move unexpectedly (as those involved in illegal pursuits often do). He was only able to take a handful of seeds with him when he relocated to California and, remarkably, one of his Jamaican Lion seeds grew into a female plant.

Shadrock works as an arborist and smokes his creation for pain relief. "I need herb that keeps me aware of where I am while relieving pain—Jamaican Lion does that," he says. "It has a cerebral effect—it's very energetic and enlightening and provides six to eight hours of pain relief for my back."

It was only many years later that he discovered what he had created. Someone had broken into his home and robbed him and he needed money to cover the rent so he went to Harborside to sell some of his Jamaican Lion harvest. When the buyer got the test results back, he put Shadrock in touch with the lab and Project

CBD. Jamaican Lion contained nearly 8 percent CBD. Since then he has been working on developing new strains based on Jamaican Lion, but he still grows primarily for himself, rarely selling any to dispensaries. And he does not sell seeds or clones. He is worried about losing control of the strain, about others taking what he considers to be his intellectual property. He is hoping to find a way to make the plant more available while retaining control, but for the time being the plant is mostly for personal consumption.

These CBD-rich strains are rare but as growers learn more about them, and an increasing amount of the marijuana sold through dispensaries is tested for THC and CBD, they are starting to be discovered. Martin Lee, co-founder of Project CBD, says that he has been in contact with about a half dozen breeders so far who have created CBD-rich strains mostly on their own without the benefit of even knowing much about CBD let alone using testing to guide their breeding process. Those most commonly available at the end of 2011 were Harlequin and Cannatonic. These and the other CBD-rich strains often have Sour Diesel or True Blueberry in their genetic lines. "The gene pools of these plants are incredibly varied," he says. "In some ways the only thing holding us back from finding more of these strains is the small number of testing labs."

Ringo, Shadrock, and growers and breeders like them are the foundation of the medical cannabis industry in California. It relies on people who have spent their lives in the illegal cannabis underground for everything from breeding to growing to providing advice to sick people. Today they are really the only ones with an in-depth knowledge of the plant here in the United States. And given the legal gray zone the plant is in today, they are likely to be the only ones in this business for some time to come. In some important ways that has hobbled the plant and the industry.

These people still have to work in much the same way they did for decades, conducting breeding programs with inadequate numbers of plants, living with a well-earned distrust of government and law enforcement, and only now able to have access to basic lab equipment that allows them to know the cannabinoid profile of the plants they are breeding. Harborside, for example, has been among those trying to find high-CBD strains and then get them to growers and breeders so they can create robust, stabilized, high-CBD strains for production. But, despite its efforts at professionalism, this important effort has run into some very amateurish problems. Jeremy Ramsay, who runs the dispensary's clone department, tells me that he was once given a True Blueberry/OG Kush plant. The strain has tested as high as 12.7 percent CBD. He gave it to one of their cloners and it died, leaving them without the genetic stock. He gave another high CBD mother to another cloner who came back weeks later with cuttings to sell. Then the cloner realized that he had given Ramsay the wrong clones and could not account for what happened to the high-CBD mother. "There have been some stumbling blocks for sure," says Ramsay.

GW Pharmaceuticals offers a radically different and radically more professional model for moving forward. The company's founder, Dr. Geoffrey Guy, who has a background in traditional pharmaceutical companies as well as those working with plant extracts, had a long-standing interest in plant-based medicine. He wanted his company to take a very different approach to developing drugs. Historically, many medicines were developed by isolating molecules found in nature—aspirin, for example, was derived from salicin, a compound found in willow bark. More recently, researchers have been creating drugs by synthesizing molecules that work with particular receptors in the brain, moving entirely away from compounds found in nature. That, Dr. Guy says, is problematic. As he explains, traditional pharmaceutical companies "synthesize a molecule never exposed to any living being on the planet and then wonder why there is toxicity or unintended pharmacological consequences." Instead, GW Pharmaceuticals is returning to the much older approach of working directly with the plant. The combination of various compounds found in plants can often complement the effect they have on people or balance out what might be a negative effect that a drug based on a single synthetic molecule might have on its own. Dr. Guy says there is evidence that the 80 cannabinoids and the terpenes work in just this way, complementing each other, balancing out extreme effects much like CBD is believed to temper the high brought on by THC. "We knew that there would be therapeutic effects from exposure to the whole plant," he says. He wanted to begin making medicine from the whole plant so patients could benefit from the large number of cannabinoids and terpenes. The problem was, how to obtain the plants?

Dr. Guy got in contact with HortaPharm, a company in Holland. HortaPharm wasn't just another struggling pharmaceutical company. It was founded by Rob Clarke and Dave Watson. Clarke is the author of *Marijuana Botany: Propagation and Breeding of Distinctive Cannabis*, one of the most scientifically oriented books on cannabis and an irreplaceable reference for many breeders. And Dave Watson, of course, brought seeds, including grow-guide author Mel Frank's seeds, to Amsterdam and was a key figure in launching Amsterdam's growing and breeding business. Each of them spent decades traveling the globe collecting cannabis seeds and likely strung together one of the most comprehensive cannabis seed libraries in the world.

But they lacked the resources to do the research required to turn these seeds into medicine. Now, there was a legitimate business knocking on their door wanting to put these genetics to work in the pharmaceutical industry. And in 1998 they obliged.

GW has a massive growing and breeding operation as well as its own processing facility where it turns dried cannabis into its sublingual spray, Sativex. As of the end of 2011 the drug was approved to treat muscle spasms associated with multiple sclerosis in Canada, the United Kingdom, Spain, Denmark, Germany, and New Zealand, and cancer pain in Canada. It expects to be approved or to launch Sativex in 14 more countries in 2012. It has also begun Phase 3 trials in the United States—the last round of trials before the drug will be considered by the FDA for approval. The company has marketing, distribution, and even research and development deals with some of the biggest names in the pharmaceutical industry including Bayer and Novartis. It's publicly traded. And it grows an incredible amount of marijuana.

Sativex's main active ingredients are THC and CBD—about a one-to-one mix of the two cannabinoids. However, the company was never able to breed a plant with equally high levels of both compounds. So Sativex is made from extracts from two different strains, one high in THC and one high in CBD. Finding a CBD-rich strain was nearly impossible at the time. David Potter, the company's director of botanical research and cultivation, explains that at one point he bought seeds on the black market from 50 different strains and only 3 percent had any CBD at all. GW bred these plants long before Ringo and others developed their CBD-rich strains, and GW has no contact with the US-based medical and underground breeders. The only way the company could get a high CBD strain was to start working with varieties bred for hemp production, which have had the THC bred out of them, allowing them to produce at least some CBD. It found a variety with 1 percent CBD and through selective breeding eventually created a strain that produces 8 percent CBD.

The THC-rich strain used in Sativex was developed from Watson's Skunk #1. Potter and the gardeners here initially planted 2000 Skunk #1 seeds—half of them were males so they were discarded. Of the remaining 1000, they kept the 30 or so that were the most rigorous high-yielding plants with the highest THC profiles. "We were going for touch and feel and smell as well as the analytical stuff," says Potter. Then over the course of a year they winnowed those down to seven plants, from which all of their Sativex production is done today. "It's a case of just growing batches and batches and batches of these things," says Potter.

GW grows its marijuana in a large, high-ceiling greenhouse. The main grow room must be 20 feet tall and the ceiling is made of glass. Three thousand marijuana plants sit on waist-high tables. Plants are moved through the room like car parts on a slow-motion assembly line. Every week a few tables full of plants are harvested at one end of the room and at the opposite end another few tables of plants are introduced. "Henry Ford would love it," says Potter. Plants spend 11 weeks in here getting 12 hours of light a day from sun shining through the glass ceiling and artificial light from high pressure sodium bulbs suspended over the tables. A computer system monitors the humidity and temperature, keeping them both constant.

The plants here are grown in soil and GW does not use pesticides. Instead it uses eight types of insects that are benign to the cannabis plants to control the population of pests that infest and feed on cannabis, an approach called integrated pest management. Here, for example, gardeners introduce small wasps that lay their eggs inside of white flies and eat their way out, killing the host. They release mites that eat the larvae of another pest.

These plants are unlike others that I've seen. Whereas most growers I have met trim their plants to focus the plant's energy on bud production, little of this goes on here. The plants look like teenagers in need of haircuts. Stalks and branches extend haphazardly out of the mass of green that reaches up towards the sky. After 11 weeks when the flowers are mature and ready to be harvested, these plants are six feet tall—much taller than most indoor plants.

GW does not worry about optimum bud production because it is not growing cannabis for anyone to smoke. Perfectly formed, dense buds dripping with trichomes are not the goal. Instead GW is producing what everyone who works there calls "Botanical Raw Material" or BRM: buds and leaves that are minced into a fine powder that is eventually turned into GW's spray.

And, here, unlike in most marijuana grows, no one is trying to coax better performance out of the plant. The company has been approved to provide Sativex in a particular formulation with a certain amount of THC and CBD (as well as the other terpenes and cannabinoids in small amounts) and every batch must be the same within certain tolerances. As cultivation director, Potter's job is not to maximize yield or turn out the highest THC strains he can. His job is to grow the same strain, the same way, over and over again so the THC and CBD levels are always the same—a monoculture assembly line of plants. In this room and a second production room, GW produces more than 30 pounds of dried BRM a day.

Once the cannabis is dried and the stems are removed, the leaves and buds are packed up in boxes and moved across the parking lot to another single-story brick building where it is processed into Sativex. THC and CBD strains are kept separate until the very end of the process. The marijuana is minced into a fine powder and then heated to activate the cannabinoids. Those cannabinoids are then extracted under high pressure using liquid carbon dioxide. GW actually uses a machine that once made extracts from hops—the cannabis plant's nearest relative. What results is a dark viscous liquid of very concentrated THC or CBD—about 70 percent pure. That liquid is then refined. Throughout various points in the process the cannabis is frozen (there are entire hallways of freezers in the building) allowing GW to keep the product at any stage of production for up to two years. Only at the end of the process are the CBD and THC extracts combined with ethanol, propylene glycol, and peppermint oil to help mask the bitter taste of the plant.

GW does its own bottling and packaging on site. Its production facility is run according to international standards and managed by someone who once managed a production facility for Pfizer. Booties, hairnets, and lab coats are worn at all times and must be changed when moving from room to room. There are no chickens wandering around here. The GW production process is as professional as most cannabis production in the United States is amateur.

In some ways GW is taking the best of both worlds—the genetic heritage of the marijuana underground and a more holistic approach of using an extract with the professionalism developed by the pharmaceutical industry—to create a product that incorporates the benefits of both. But GW has become incredibly controversial among medical marijuana advocates. Activists have used studies by GW to bolster their own claims for marijuana's effectiveness. And GW is not pleased. The company has asked organizations to stop quoting its studies. There is no relationship between a joint and Sativex, says Justin Gover, GW's managing director. "This is not some cannabis being grown on a hillside out in northern California and then being ground up. This is different," says Gover. "I can see why there are connections made between the two, but there is a very different process we go through. The whole point of modern medicine has been to try to safeguard patients. The way in which medicines are developed and regulated, you wind up with a better world."

GW is bringing a level of professionalism to breeding, growing, and applying the plant to medical research that has been missing. The staff here has the potential to bend the plant much further towards its therapeutic potential than breeders like Ringo, if only because GW's breeders are working hand in hand with those conducting medical research—tailoring the plant to the researcher's every need. GW has also put its intellectual property stamp on the plant. Since Sativex is based on plant extracts, GW cannot patent the drug itself. Instead it protects its intellectual property by obtaining plant breeders' rights for the strains of cannabis that it uses in Sativex. In order to get this protection— one commonly applied to legal crops in Europe—it had to prove that the strain is distinct, uniform, and stable. The grant protects the company's rights to the plant for 18 years. This does not preclude anyone else from developing high CBD or THC strains, just from using the exact same strains that GW is using. This kind of legal protection for a cannabis strain is a large step towards the normal business practices that other plants are subject to and certainly emphasizes the kind of quality breeding that the Canadian breeder Chimera would approve of. Yet GW remains a sort of bogeyman for many who pioneered the development of the plant. Some have told me that GW is the Monsanto of cannabis. They fear that it will monopolize the plant, tie up strains with legal barriers, making it illegal for others to grow their high-THC and high-CBD strains. They worry that the company plans to take medical marijuana away from the decentralized network of underground growers and breeders and place it firmly in the hands of a publicly traded pharmaceutical company. Dr. Guy thinks that is nothing more than a paranoid fantasy, noting that his plant breeders' rights are limited to a handful out of thousands of strains. Dr. Guy's inability to understand these fears may well stem from the incredible gulf that exists between GW's manufacturing facility with its lab coats, hair nets, and clinical acronyms and the groundswell of adoration for the plant among enthusiasts in places like California. The two approaches to the plant are so vastly different that it is hard to comprehend that GW's lab and the Cannabis Cup, for example, are dedicated to the very same plant.

9 THE CANNABIS GOLD RUSH IS ON

Inside a conference center on the outskirts of San Francisco's South of Market neighborhood, rows of booths are set up, much like you'd see at a technology conference or car show. Eager entrepreneurs are seated behind stacks of brochures and product samples ready with a sales pitch. But here the people in booths are not pitching the latest smartphone or electric car. Instead, they are hawking high-tech smoking devices—bowls, bongs, vaporizers—as well as lights for indoor growing, organic plant nutrients, books, photographs, just about anything you can think of that is marijuana-related, including marijuana itself along with hash and edibles like cookies and brownies laced with marijuana. The San Francisco Medical Cannabis Cup, organized by *High Times* magazine, is a celebration of all things cannabis.

The magazine organizes a similar event in Colorado—but *High Times* has hardly cornered the market. This event competes with Hempcon, the Kush Expo, the Colorado Cannabis

Convention, THC Expose, and the International Cannabis and Hemp Expo, to name a few. Like many of these events, the San Francisco Medical Cannabis Cup is part trade show, part conference, and part pot smoker's paradise.

Despite marijuana's counterculture roots, the strategy these entrepreneurs use to attract attention to their products is not much different from those employed at other trade shows. Throughout the vast conference center, scantily clad young women stand in front of the booths passing out fliers and brochures and chatting up potential customers.

In front of a promotional booth for Bhang Chocolate, a woman wearing tiny shorts and a cinched-up shirt has a sticker on her backside that reads "Wanna Bhang?" The company, which is named after a traditional Indian beverage that includes cannabis, sells six different kinds of chocolate bars—milk chocolate, toffee, a spicy bar, two dark chocolate bars, and one with pretzels in it. The chocolate bars contain between 60 mg and 120 mg of cannabis extract depending on the bar. Here, inside the conference center, they cannot actually sell the bars so this booth is simply to promote the brand.

Scott Van Rixel, the company's owner, may well be the only person at the cannabis cup wearing a blazer. He is not an old hand at the marijuana industry like many here. Instead, he comes from the conventional business world. He is a former chef turned chocolatier. He and his brother own the Chocolate Cartel, a gourmet chocolate company based in New Mexico that makes truffles, chocolate bars, and hot chocolate mixes. Chocolate Cartel gelato is sold at Whole Foods. Van Rixel tells me that he saw a big opening in the market for edibles—food laced with marijuana sold at medical dispensaries. "A lot of edibles are not prepared in a professional kitchen, they don't have nutritional information, ingredient lists, calorie counts," he says. "We want to bring legitimacy to the industry. We want to do things right from the beginning and work from standards put out by the FDA," standards used for food products.

Van Rixel opened Bhang in Oakland to be able to service the huge medicinal marijuana market in California. His bars are wrapped in professionally printed packaging—they would not look out of place near his gelato at Whole Foods. He tests the strength of the cannabis going into his bars so consumers will have an accurate sense of how much of the drug they are dosing themselves with. The world of cannabis, he says, could use some professionalizing. The change is inevitable and as an experienced entrepreneur from the non-cannabis culinary world, he thinks his culinary and business experience gives him a head start when it comes to legitimizing marijuana-laced foods. So far, he has been doing well. His "Triple Strength Fire Bar" won second place at this event two years in a row.

While we talk, he pauses to take a picture of the girl with the Bhang sticker on her lower back. "I'm not just making an excuse to take a picture of your ass," he tells her jokingly. He needs to send the image to his attorney who is unhappy with the company's racy promotional efforts.

This event is divided into two distinct parts. Inside are companies like Bhang and those hawking lights, paraphernalia, and other items involved in the growing, smoking, and consuming of marijuana. Outside is where you can actually buy and smoke pot. But in order to go outside, where dispensaries are selling marijuana, hash, edibles, and tinctures and where breeders are selling their seeds, you need a card proving that you are a medical marijuana patient. That, as I soon discover, is easily done.

The first booth I find is run by the Kush Clinic. Several young women are working at a table and have me fill out a few forms. I explain that I am not a California resident. This, apparently, is not a problem. After waiting around for a few minutes I am led around the corner to see the doctor.

Sitting at a card table behind a laptop computer is Dr. Howard Ragland Jr. The tight curls of his Afro poke out from beneath his baseball hat. He's wearing a t-shirt and his beard is unkempt. He tells me that he works in Long Beach and that many soldiers suffering from post-traumatic stress disorder show up at his clinic seeking recommendations for medical marijuana. They are unhappy with the side effects of the prescription medication provided by the government, he says. He asks me what my condition is. Really, my only condition is that I want to go outside to see the other part of the event.

"Sleep," I say. It's more word association than any description of an ailment. Actually, on the rare occasions that I have smoked marijuana, I want to go to sleep, almost instantly. Drowsiness is more the problem I get from smoking marijuana, not a problem that I need cured by it, though there certainly are times when I have had trouble sleeping.

The doctor nods without looking up from his laptop and sends me back out to the women at the table out front. They take my $60, take my picture, and print out a photo ID card for me. Then they hand me a manila envelope with my medical recommendation—a form from the California Department of Public Heath filled out by the doctor that includes his name, address, and California medical license number. On the form there is a list of 12 possible reasons for getting a medical marijuana recommendation: AIDS, anorexia, arthritis, cachexia (wasting syndrome), cancer, chronic pain, glaucoma, migraine, persistent muscle spasms, seizures, severe nausea, and "other." Next to this

Dr. Ragland has written in a physician's barely legible scrawl: insomnia.

It's not exactly clear what the Kush Clinic is, whether it's a dispensary, a doctor's office, or a storefront. I determine later that it has no webpage and is based in Visalia, a tiny town in California's central valley, south of Fresno. Dr. Ragland, who, according to the Medical Board of California, is a Los Angeles–based obstetrician, appears to be affiliated with companies that offer marijuana recommendations from Long Beach to San Jose—advertising recommendations for as little as $35, and a free one if you bring in three friends. Regardless of where he actually practices medicine, the card Kush Clinic issued on his recommendation is all that's needed to get me through the doors to the "215 Medicating Area," the designated pot buying and smoking zone named after the number of the ballot measure—Proposition 215—that allowed the medical use of marijuana back in 1996.

In the years since then, and particularly over the last few years, California has become the destination for those in the marijuana business. In towns throughout Humboldt and Mendocino counties, stores that sell everything needed to cultivate marijuana indoors or outdoors seem to be more prevalent than gas stations. With the demise of the timber and fishing industries, growing marijuana is about all that is left. No one knows for sure how much marijuana is grown in California. A 2006 estimate by Jon Gettman, an assistant professor of Criminal Justice at Shenandoah University and a former director of NORML, put California's total annual crop (medical and illegal) at $14 billion—making it the state's most valuable agricultural product, worth twice as much as the runner up, the dairy industry, and seven times as valuable as the wine industry. Gettman's numbers, like all of the data about the cannabis industry, are extrapolations. No one knows for sure how much marijuana is grown in the United States. All that is known is how much is confiscated and eradicated. Gettman uses these government statistics along with estimates of usage to determine the size of the crop. These figures are an estimate, but it is all that researchers have to go on. And, says Gettman, given the massive growth of the industry in California since he published his report, the annual crop is certainly much larger than it was in 2006. The Rand Corporation estimates that as much as a million pounds of marijuana a year is consumed in state and, according to Dale Gieringer, state director of California NORML, that is just a fraction of the amount harvested here every year. One research firm, See Change Strategy, estimated that the entire US medical cannabis market was worth $1.7 billion in 2011 and could double in the next five years. California's medical market, with dispensaries, grow stores, and growers across the state, is already leading this quasi-legal, cannabis-driven economy.

Nomaad (who asked that I use his industry moniker rather than his real name) is one of those who moved here to make a new life for himself and a living in the cannabis industry. I meet Nomaad at a one-story, two-bedroom house on a narrow road in rural Lake County, east of Mendocino County. The house is hidden behind a tall fence and a large metal gate is swung open across the driveway. The house is sparsely furnished. There is a long sectional against one wall in the living room and a table and chairs pushed up against another. There are no beds, though there's a sleeping bag on the floor in one room. The back bedroom has a desk with a computer and three chairs. A bong stands on the floor next to one of the chairs. The house is at once thoroughly lived in and completely abandoned. The reason quickly becomes apparent: the only full-time tenants here are the 99 marijuana plants growing in three large greenhouses out back.

Nomaad tells me he grew up on Long Island and worked on movies and on reality TV shows for many years before he finally got fed up with the industry. In 2004 he moved his family to Costa Rica and taught himself to build custom bamboo houses. He was making a good living at it until the US housing market crashed and customers who used to show up with $100,000 in cash to build their dream home started to disappear. He started to think about what else he might do to earn a living. "I've always been a smoker and I've always sold to smoke," Nomaad tells me, and because of that he has had connections here for years.

So, Nomaad saved up $12,000 and moved his family to Lake County. When he got here, he started talking to other growers and visiting their gardens. "I just kind of hung out with my friends. It's a hanging-out business," he says after taking a long hit on the bong that he keeps near the desk. Growers are always interested in how their friends are growing, the different techniques and approaches they use. "I have three people a week come through my garden and then I go out and see their gardens the next month." The best growers, he noticed, all used huge planters. Over time growers have realized that most strains of cannabis plants spread their roots wide rather than deep so the bigger the pot—some hold hundreds of gallons of soil—the better. "That's what's fun about it," he says. "Nobody went to school for this, yet everyone is an expert to their own degree. I love that knowledge exchange."

Nomaad turns on his computer. Unlike the previous generation of growers who refuse to keep any records, Nomaad is an obsessive record keeper. In part it is because he is fairly comfortable with the legal acceptance of his grow—he tells me the sheriff has been here to make sure that he is adhering to local law. But he also keeps records because it is the only way to be able to understand how well your business is doing. It is necessary to be able to improve growing techniques year to year, troubleshoot problems, understand and manage annual expenses, and, ultimately, understand how much money one is actually making. Nomaad uses Google Calendars to keep records of everything he does with the plants year after year. He also has photographs on his computer of each plant through its grow cycle. He uses a proxy server to get to the information and his entire operating system is encrypted.

This is his third year growing here, in Lake County. He shows me last year's calendar. It's color coded—orange is for the light deprivation crop (a technique outdoor growers use to trick plants into flowering early) and purple is for the rest of the crop. He can look up exactly what he did with each plant on any given day. Then he scrolls through thousands of images of plants, each one tagged so he knows when he took the shot and what strain the plant is. Some of the plants that he photographed near harvest in the fall are so large they tower over his head. "It's a real business now," he says. "And organized wins—every time."

Nomaad can't grow these plants on his own. Moving soil, potting and transplanting plants, watering, feeding with nutrients, all of that can be very labor intensive. And, as in any business, finding good help is not easy. "Just last week we got rid of a guy. I had him carrying bags of dirt and he was like, 'I didn't know this was going to be a lot of work,'" he says. "These are just the most entitled schmucks, trust fund kids like 28 years old and they think they are doing something but they are not doing it well. Like on 'American Idol,' I weed people out."

Nomaad walks me through his greenhouses, first showing me

the plants he plans to use for the light deprivation crop. His greenhouse is filled with these plants, representing half a dozen strains—OG Kush, Blue Dragon, Blue Kush, Grape Stomper, Blackberry Kush, and Sour Diesel, all just a few feet tall. In another domed greenhouse, the thick musty smell of marijuana is powerful. Nomaad looks over the rows of plants, pointing out their broad leaves. They are Chem Dog, OG Kush, and Sour Diesel strains. "These are all related to each other," he says. "And they are the hottest strains right now. That's because they get you more high and they taste amazing."

Finding the right strain to grow is one of the keys to success. Not only do growers have to grow, harvest, and prepare the marijuana perfectly, but if it's not the right strain, then they may not find someone to sell it to. Even then, Nomaad says, growers can still lose money. Standing outside looking at the massive pots that his plants will be transplanted into next month, he says that losing money is just part of being in this business. "I've lost more at this business than I've made at three other businesses combined," he says. Part of the reason is because the market is flooded with marijuana. In 2005 high-quality marijuana whole-saled for as much as $4000 a pound. In 2011 some reported receiving as little as $1200 a pound. In the past, dealers on the black market were desperate for product. Now, roles are reversed and dealers can set the terms. "Let's say you sell 20 pounds of weed for $50,000 dollars," says Nomaad. "And then you just never see the money—it's gone, for one of a thousand reasons. It's not like it's rare. It's like, one in three. You put 60 pounds out on the road, you are going to lose 20 pounds. People in this industry think herb is money. They think that on Thanksgiving Day they are going to have $200,000. No, on Thanksgiving Day you are going to have a hundred pounds of weed, my friend."

And as a result of that, Nomaad says, growers live in a strange financial world. He tells me that the first preference for purchasing anything is to pay in marijuana and because of that people who accept payment in marijuana charge much more. People pay double the value of something if they can pay for it in marijuana, he says. After paying in marijuana, the second preference is cash, and people pay a premium here for things they can buy in cash too. The Humboldt Growers Association's Joey Burger, for example, owns a shop called Trimscene that sells machines to trim buds. Nomaad says that you can buy the machines for thousands of dollars less online but that people gladly pay Burger a premium because they can pay in cash. The last thing anyone wants to do is use a credit card. With lots of off-the-books income it can be hard to get credit cards, and they create a paper trail.

For Nomaad the key to making this business work is having enough money on hand to be able to hold his crop until the spring. When the large outdoor crop is harvested in the fall, the market is flooded. Prices go down. It's harder to sell. Like many growers, he uses a machine that seals the marijuana in bags that are filled with nitrogen to forestall oxidation, which can cause the buds to dry out and get stale. That way the buds can be sold later when there is less marijuana on the market and prices are higher.

Even though Nomaad is new to the business, he does not have much faith that the business will last. More and more people are growing and flooding the market with marijuana. With the possibility of legalization, he thinks larger, better-funded businesses will get involved. Seed companies will be taken over by big corporations with high-tech breeding operations that will undercut the hundreds of independents. "I don't think this business has another decade. It's eroding in so many ways at once," he says. "I would love to see it work out long term. I would love to be in this business in 20 years, a vibrant business where I could market my herb nationwide like wine."

Then he pauses, looks around at his yard, the greenhouses, the massive pots awaiting their plants, the run-down house that anchors the operation. "There is just craziness in this business, constantly. We don't know what's going to happen to the prices every year," he says. "The only thing we know for sure is that there's going to be more weed."

Several hours north of Nomaad's grow operation, I meet Luke (who does not tell me his full name). His uncombed red hair juts out at odd angles and hangs down into his eyes. He's got a barely visible patchy red beard. We meet in the food coop in Arcata, a huge supermarket with a deli and bakery and tables up front for those dining in. It looks more like a Whole Foods than a cooperative. Luke tells me that he knew nothing about growing marijuana when he moved here. He came to Humboldt from the Midwest to go to business school. But as he watched the economy sink into recession and heard his friends tell him about having to move back in with their parents after college because they could not find jobs, he began to think twice about the debt load he'd be taking on in graduate school. "We were the recipients of the promise of the American dream," he says. "But that all fell apart."

Slowly, Luke found himself drawn into the local cannabis culture. He began volunteering at the Humboldt Patient Resource Center, an Arcata dispensary that encourages people to come in and volunteer to help out with the plants. In exchange they get a remarkable education from the cultivation director, Kevin Jodrey, as well as from long-time growers who drop in and other gardeners there. And Luke spent lots of time on online forums like those run by International Cannagraphic on its website ICMag.com.

The company's logo looks a bit like a marijuana-tinged spoof of *National Geographic*. It features news stories and hosts online discussion forums where experienced growers often share tips and help others troubleshoot problems. "You get pockets of really high-end growers, they don't fuck around," says Luke. "You get incredible in-depth discussions, like high-level scientific discussion of what is going on with plants or certain strains or the particular lineage."

Luke is not the kind of person I expected to find growing cannabis for a living. He is a devout Catholic. He regularly attends church. He thinks that global warming is a conspiracy drummed up by scientists and the government. When I mention that most growers I meet are men and question why so few women grow, he tells me that women are usually trimmers and that some growers make their trimmers work topless. Though he thinks that making women work topless is a bit over the creepy sexist line, he says that he is a fan of gender roles in general. "People in our society don't like to hear that, but a person can draw identity from these roles, a purpose," he tells me. "The women seem to like it and if they don't they can do something about it." Luke is definitely not your stereotypical hippy who's run off to the woods to grow pot.

We get in Luke's black pickup truck and drive south towards Eureka. Along the way he points out the Jack Daniels billboard that reads: "Jack Daniels, The Number Seven Seed" (which seems to be a weirdly localized ad campaign targeting those who know the value of a rare strain of seeds) and the Budweiser billboard—"Grab Some Buds"—a national campaign that takes on added significance here. We turn off the highway and pass a self-storage facility that advertises the availability of secure, temperature- and humidity-controlled units (a barely concealed pitch to those looking to rent a grow room) and turn into a small complex of two-story townhouses. Luke takes me upstairs and into a unit at the end of the row facing the back of the complex.

Despite the fact that a friend of Luke's lives here, the apartment has the same lived-in and abandoned feeling as Nomaad's house. The kitchen table has no chairs around it; instead, they are lined up against the wall in the living room. A blanket is on the floor next to the couch and an ironing board stands in the hallway. "I berate him endlessly for his apartment," says Luke.

He leads me down the hallway to the spare bedroom. The overhead light is broken. Inside there are two tall black grow tents. These are rectangular black boxes about six feet tall. They have holes on either side for attaching ventilation systems and zippers down the front. Luke opens one. It is lined with highly reflective Mylar and gives off a bright glare.

Inside, eight trays, each containing dozens of tiny marijuana plants, sit on metal shelves beneath lights. The plants, cuttings from the mother plants in the next tent over, are about six inches tall. The cuttings were made eight days earlier. But not all is well. The leaves of most of the plants in one of the trays have turned brown. Some have withered completely. "I'll probably just throw this whole tray out," Luke says sounding disappointed. He is not sure what the problem was. The tray was full of the weakest clones, but nonetheless he's upset that more than $500 worth of plants will wind up in the garbage. Perhaps there was not enough ventilation, he ventures. "I'll have to sit down with my partners and figure out what went wrong," he says. On the bright side, the remaining trays of healthy clones will bring in anywhere from $3000 to $6000 before expenses.

Luke unzips the adjacent tent to reveal several mother plants clustered under grow lights. They are West Coast Dog, a nearly odorless strain, and a few others mixed in as well. The plants are tall and narrow, a result of having been cut back for clone production. Luke may let some of these flower to harvest the marijuana. He'll keep others for making more clones. If he uses this tent to flower the plants, he says that he can expect to harvest about two pounds or maybe a little more of dried buds. That can bring in about $5000. Combining flowering with the clone operation, he can bring close to $10,000 every two months from this spare bedroom before paying for electricity and supplies.

Luke does not grow for himself. He is essentially a contract grower—a surprising niche career in the marijuana cultivation world. Luke and those like him will essentially plant, grow, and harvest the crop for someone else on their property in exchange for a cut of the profits. The grower does the work, the property owner (or renter as in this case), manages the relationships with dispensaries and ensures that their paperwork is in order. They carry the risk of having the marijuana on their property, the grower does the work, and they divide the profits. This is just one of several grow operations that Luke manages. Luke says that he really enjoys the work. Though he never worked with plants before and had little exposure to illegal drugs, he is drawn to the culture of growing and the odd work schedule that these plants demand. Some days are full of hard work—16 hours a day transplanting, harvesting, trimming. There are times when the work is non-stop. As much as you can fit in, you can do. And then there are long stretches when the plants are simply growing and there is little to do. He usually comes by to water this grow a few times a week—since these plants are clones and mothers, they do not need to be watered as regularly as those in flower. Much of the work of growing, particularly if you are trying to grow for others as Luke is, involves socializing, making connections, trying to find the right people to do business with. "Nine-tenths of my time this time of year is social," Luke says. "It's talking with people, try-ing to put things together, trying to see what is happening, when packages of marijuana are going out, what the cut is going to be, when I am going to get paid. The social is constant."

And, of course, there is the worry about getting arrested, even here. While small-scale growers are generally left alone, there are still plenty of busts of large-scale growers and even some small-time ones. Despite the general tolerance of small-scale growing here and in Mendocino County, in 2010 the federal government confiscated more marijuana in California than it has in any pre-vious year. According to the DEA, 7.4 million plants were seized in 2010 (70 percent of all the plants seized in the United States that year were seized in California). Most of that was from raids on massive growing operations in national forests. But growers are always a bit wary. Luke tells me that while he was at this clone operation with two friends, there was a knock at the door. He opened it to find a Jehovah's Witness. "That was really stressful," he says. "You worry about it. If you are in southern Humboldt and you hear a helicopter go overhead, you think, 'Am I about to get hit with something serious? Is shit about to go down? What are my folks going to say?'"

Luke and I get back in his pickup truck for the drive back to Arcata. As he pulls out onto the highway, he lights up a joint. "You have to be careful when you drive here," he tells me as he lets out a stream of marijuana smoke. Gesturing at the passing cars, he says. "You should always assume that everyone is high."

Growers like Luke who comply with state law or are small enough to avoid much attention are still breaking federal law. For Luke, and other growers, there is always some risk of arrest. But, at the events where cannabis is celebrated, like the one in San Francisco, caution is left completely at the door. Smokers, growers, breeders, everyone here who leads a part of their life in secrecy, can come to this place and dispense with their fears.

And they certainly are in the Cannabis Cup's "215 Medicating Area" where only those with patient cards can go. It is so crowded that it's hard to move. About a dozen different dispensaries have booths here. Some are elaborate affairs with DJs, sitting areas, and cannabis plants. Others are just tables behind which people are selling various strains of marijuana, different types of hash, and edibles including cakes, cookies, and even drinks. Another sells parts that you can use to turn apples, pears, and other fruit into smoking devices. The crowd in front of Ken Estes' Grand Daddy Purp booth is vast.

At the table run by a seed company called OG Genetics, two large men with buzzed hair and crisp baseball hats are explaining the various types of seeds that they have available to a small crowd of people. Both have elaborate tattoos in large gothic letters running up their arms and peeking out above the necks of their shirts. John, who runs the operation, which is based in Riverside, says that he has been breeding for five years. He produces mostly hybrids bred with OG Kush. His company sells seeds and clones and will even build a grow room for you.

Around the corner, I run into a man with a three-foot-long glass pipe. The bowl, about the size of a cereal bowl, is stuffed with what must be a several ounces of marijuana. A crowd has gathered around him and he gladly passes the comically immense pipe from one person to the next.

As I'm about to leave, I run into the southern Humboldt breeder Lawrence Ringo. I almost didn't see him. Whereas most people out here are doing their best to draw attention, get noticed, sell product, Ringo is hard to find. He's pushed his chair back from his table and is involved in a lengthy conversation. The banner for his seed company is strung so low over the booth that you have to duck your head under it to get close enough to him to talk. In this buzzing world of cannabis business, Ringo is not so much lost as he is ambivalent—interested enough to show up, but hardly willing to pitch himself like so many of the other eager seed purveyors.

Ringo is sharing space with a company called Pure Analytics. They test his marijuana, and the young plants that he is considering breeding, for potency, checking for levels of CBD, CBN, CBG, and THC. Samantha Miller, who runs the company, has been doing this since 2010. Miller tells me that she grew up around the industry in northern California, but she's not like most of the entrepreneurs or smokers working the booths or wandering the floor. Her hair is pulled back into a tight ponytail. She wears wire-rimmed glasses and speaks in a quick, thoughtful way. She shunned the industry when she was young. Instead, she pursued advanced degrees in science and a career in high tech. She worked for biotech and pharmaceutical companies for 15 years. But, after working in that world for so long, she was hungry for a new challenge.

After talking with friends in the business, she realized that there was a big need that wasn't being met. At the time there were few companies offering legitimate testing of cannabis. As more research comes out showing the medicinal benefits of strains that are high in CBD and CBN, more growers and dispensaries have been interested in finding out how much of those compounds are in the strains they are selling. And they want to communicate that to patients. Of course, for those looking to get high, big THC numbers are also a huge selling point.

Miller realized that she had the skills and management know-how to run such an operation—at one time she even worked for one of the companies that make the gas chromatography machines that test for these compounds. She quit her job and went into business. Abandoning her career was a tough decision. She knew that by jumping into the world of medical marijuana, she would be burning her ties to the conventional world of high-tech and pharmaceutical companies. If this failed, she would have a very hard time going back to her old profession. "Just Google my name and marijuana or my company name," says Miller. "I can never hide what I've been doing."

When she started, she says that there were four companies that provided this service in the entire state. "Now there are fifteen, and those are just the ones that I know of," she tells me. "In Michigan there are five—imagine, five—in Michigan alone."

The problem with this boom, she says, is that many of the people getting into the testing business lack the scientific skills required to run a lab that turns out consistently accurate results. Bad results tarnish the entire testing industry. That is one of the downsides of the old marijuana world meeting the new one, she says. "This is a DIY industry," she says. "And these companies are just taking advantage of it." Anyone can buy a machine and get trained to use it, she says, even if they don't understand the kinds of process and procedures required to do such complex testing. Marco, the San Francisco grower, even bought one of these machines at a Silicon Valley garage sale—of course it did not come with a manual or training course. If these companies start releasing bad or inconsistent results, everyone suffers. And since there is no regulation of cannabis itself—no one requires any level of quality or production process or labeling—there is no one to step in and police these testing companies.

Ringo says that Miller has not only been reliable in her testing but a real help in spreading the word about his high-CBD strains: "She is the most awesome person in this business you'll meet. She goes around to these dispensaries on weekends and gives seminars and hips them up to what CBDs are and what they do."

Miller hopes that her reliability and her rigorous approach will help her prevail. She really doesn't have many options. By becoming so vocal—speaking at conferences and in dispensaries, by joining a trade group of testing organizations, blogging, and being quoted in the press—she has created a long online trail tying her to this once underground industry. As she well understands, going back to her old career is not an option. For her, like many taking the leap into this unpredictable quasi-legal business, the only way is forward. Standing at her booth surrounded by thousands of people getting high and celebrating cannabis out in the open, the scientist turned cannabis entrepreneur tells me: "I took a chance. It's like driving off a cliff."

10 A DAY IN THE DISPENSARY

The Humboldt Patient Resource Center is just a few blocks from the main square in Arcata, an attractive small town dotted with Victorian-era buildings and small businesses like bakeries, coffee shops, and art galleries. The windows in the long, low dispensary building are blacked out and a blind is drawn over the glass in the door, giving an odd air of secrecy to what is ostensibly a business that dispenses medicine. Inside is a small waiting area and a counter, behind which a woman sits perched on a stool. Behind her are shelves stocked with bags of various strains of marijuana and small, young plants no more than 10 inches tall—clones cut from mother plants that are ready to be sold to growers. On a nearby shelf are cookies, brownies, and other edibles, all laced with cannabis.

Many dispensaries operate a bit like jewelry stores: the customer stands on one side of the counter looking over the selection and the clerk pulls out samples from inside a glass case for the customer to examine. This dispensary is different: only those looking to quickly buy their marijuana seem to stay in the front room. Others who the clerk determines are cooperative members with valid medical recommendations, just walk through the door next to the counter and come into the back room where the marijuana and plants are displayed. Here they can get a better look at the clones and they can talk to Kevin Jodrey, who runs the extensive growing operation here. Jodrey gladly dispenses advice, knowledge, industry gossip, and a constant stream of chatter with customers. He helps them figure out what strains they might like, what type of strains grow best where—indoors, in a greenhouse, outside in the shade, or on a south-facing hillside. He also helps growers troubleshoot problems with pests, mold, and poor yield. He spends so much time talking with customers these days—and so little actually working hands-on with the plants—that he is considering secretly switching his days off so that he can sneak in and work with the plants one day a week when customers won't come in to talk with him. Largely because of Jodrey, this place feels more like a community center than a business—a gathering place for those whose community is marijuana.

Jodrey is no casual grower. Though incredibly friendly and enthusiastic about his crop, he's not particularly casual about anything. Jodrey is compact and powerful. When we meet, he's wearing a black t-shirt with a picture of a muscle-bound pit bull with a barbell chained around its neck—the logo of Westside Barbell, a manufacturer of weightlifting equipment. The 45-year-old Jodrey is a master coach for kettlebell lifting and his son is a national champion. Jodrey grew up in Rhode Island, which comes across instantly in his sharp, nasally, rapid-fire New England accent. He began growing on the east coast and then moved out to California in the early 1990s. At first he moved to the San Francisco Bay Area where he did some indoor growing and worked construction. When a construction job brought him up to Humboldt, he decided to stay and began managing grow operations for others.

When Jodrey talks about the decades during which he grew marijuana for the illegal market, he is fast and focused. "I was just a wingnut," he says. "I was so hungry that I was obsessed, possessed was the joke." Jodrey worked on every type of grow operation he could find: indoor, hydroponic, outdoor, and greenhouse grows—organic and chemical grows. He had clients all over the area and the work was constant. "I was on the grow, baby," he says. "If you wanted to check me out, you had to meet me in between scenes." He grew in homes and in business and industrial areas. He changed his outfits so he fit in wherever he happened to be tending these indoor grows. "I had to change clothes so I could go to these projects because I was lighting up houses all over the place." It didn't take Jodrey long to realize that he had found his niche. "To me it's a craft," he says of growing marijuana. "It requires diligence and hard work and perseverance."

Now Jodrey works only in the medical marijuana business. And he has found his place as a sort of cannabis camp counselor. He has an open door policy: anyone who becomes a member of the cooperative can come in and volunteer their time working with the plants. About 10 people volunteer at any given time. He mentors the volunteers, using his decades of growing experience to help them learn how to grow on their own.

Jodrey agreed to let me volunteer for a day to learn more about the day-to-day experience of tending to the plant. When I arrive on a summer morning, Jodrey leads me into the main grow room, which is filled with over a thousand plants and lit by the sharp glare of 54 high-pressure sodium lights. The potted plants are all sitting on waist-high tables so the newly forming buds stretching up towards the lights overhead begin sprouting at about eye level. The room is warm and smells musty and skunky, yet the air is surprisingly dry thanks to dehumidifiers. Though we're inside, there is a slight breeze and a constant hum from the fans that circulate fresh air over the leaves. Navigating between the tables, past hundreds of leafy plants, is like being lost in a dense, green jungle of flowering marijuana.

Through the canopy of plants, I see the grower, Luke, whom I met earlier. Given that he learned his trade volunteering here, I'm not surprised to see him working in the flowering room this morning. Despite the cool weather outside, he's wearing shorts, a t-shirt, and sunglasses and is already breaking a sweat. He shows me how to use stakes to give the plants added support. Marijuana plants have been bred to produce such a large volume of buds that, like factory-farmed chickens that have trouble walking because they have such huge breasts, these plants cannot support themselves. The plants need to be staked so that as the buds mature, they don't break the stem that supports them. Handing me a packet of zip ties, Luke reminds me not to cinch the plants to the stakes too tightly which could pinch the stalk and cut off the flow of water and nutrients to the buds. "Never forget that each of these plants is worth a lot of money," he says for the second time that morning.

Each plant is in a square pot and 15 pots are grouped together in large rectangular trays. Luke tells me to grab some of the three-foot-long bamboo poles from a garbage can in the middle of the room and head over to the corner where a group of Purple Nepal plants are growing. The plants, some of the younger ones in the room, are over two feet tall and just beginning to flower.

Using zip ties, I begin cinching the upper stalks of the plants to the stakes. As I begin to work, I soon understand why Luke is sweating. Despite the fans, the whole room is warmed from the heat of the grow lights. With the hum of the fans in the background, it's hard to hear or be heard by the other volunteers in the farther reaches of the room so I just settle in working on the plants—eyeing the stems, trying to decide which stalks to tie up and where, whether to use one or two stakes. The task takes over and these plants—illicit and very valuable—begin to lose their cachet. In the monotony of working on one after another, they become just plants.

All of the 1200 or so plants in the room are in some stage of their roughly 60-day flowering cycle. The city of Arcata requires the dispensary to grow all of its own marijuana. It produces about 14 pounds of cured marijuana a month and must produce that much every month to come close to meeting the demand from the 2000 or so patients who are members of the cooperative. These days 14 pounds a month is not enough says Mariellen Jurkovich, the dispensary's director. She has begun to put restrictions on how much patients can buy at one time so the dispensary will have enough marijuana to go around.

Jodrey uses only organic nutrients and soil additives and no chemical pesticides or fungicides. But he hasn't always grown that way. Over the decades he grew with chemicals, he would give the plants an organic wash to eliminate any of the residual chemicals in the plant. That technique—giving plants a flood of water to flush the nutrients out of the plants as they near their harvest time—is proving important, even with the organically grown marijuana he produces today. Organic nutrients for plants are primarily fish, kelp, and beet sugar. "Everyone who is smoking organic marijuana and is saying, 'I love the flavor,' what they are really loving is the taste of beet sugar," he says.

That flavor is important. When he was young, he says the marijuana he smoked from overseas had distinct flavors that you don't find anymore. "You actually tasted Colombian dirt, Mexican dirt, Thai dirt," he says. "You tasted the place. You tasted the marijuana. Now, you taste a wash." His solution is to add his own special ingredient to his wash: molasses. "It will create the perception that the pot is what they want it to be. We can use the most organic earth ever created, but if it doesn't have that molassesy flavor, it won't taste 'earthy.'"

Regardless of the organic techniques and products that Jodrey uses to grow here, he can never call his crop organic. Since marijuana remains illegal at the federal level, it cannot be certified as organic by the government, even if it is produced in accordance with the government's guidelines. Instead, the dispensary is certified by an independent program called Clean Green, which requires those that receive its seal of approval to produce marijuana using organic standards. Jurkovich says that it is particularly important to avoid potentially harmful chemicals when growing medicine for patients, some of whom may have compromised immune systems or increased sensitivity to chemicals. It's important enough that the dispensary sacrifices income to do so. Marijuana plants grown indoors without chemicals yield about one-third less than those grown with chemicals, Jodrey says.

Since Jodrey joined the dispensary as its horticulture director in late 2009, he has completely changed the growing operation here. He created a large cloning business, helping to generate desperately needed income for the dispensary. Since the dispensary gives away about 20 percent of its marijuana to low-income members and has 11 employees, all of whom receive health insurance, its expenses are significant. Thanks to his decades of experience in the underground market, Jodrey has contacts he can call on to help him better understand what strains are popular and hence what clones growers are going to want. That way he can ramp up production on the right strain at the right time of year. He is also an avid collector of rare seeds and plants, a passion of his that can be very helpful to those patients who find relief only with rare or unpopular strains. "They call him a clone whore," says Jurkovich. His decades of growing experience have been an incredible asset to both the dispensary and to the volunteers who come here to learn the trade—something that would have been unheard of just a few years ago when growers were far more secretive. "Kevin's been essential," says Luke. "The guy is like the Yoda of marijuana."

Upstairs, where the dispensary keeps its clones and mother plants, Jodrey shows me a small plastic bag containing about two dozen seeds. They are from a strain developed by a local breeder—a cross of Big Bud (Skunk #1 crossed with Afghani) and Blue Dream (a cross of Blueberry and Super Silver Haze). The breeder is going to prison and passed the seeds to a friend, who then passed them along to Jodrey to grow in order to see how the plants and buds come out.

"These are two heavyweight strains, so maybe something big and good will come out of it," Jodrey says.

We sit down at a card table and Jodrey dumps the tiny beige and brown striped seeds into the kind of small paper tray that you'd get french fries in at a fast food restaurant. He mixes a small jar with a water and kelp solution, which helps with germination.

"Try to pick the ones that are the fattest with the most stripes," he says. "Those seeds are the most mature and have the best likelihood of germinating."

We take turns picking seeds out and dropping them into the small jar where they bob on the surface. Jodrey will let them sit overnight. By tomorrow morning those that are going to germinate will split and sink to the bottom. The rest will remain floating on the top. Jodrey will then remove those seeds that have split from the jar, wash them, and set them in a small pot of soil about one-eighth of an inch below the surface where they will begin to set down roots. In three to four weeks, he'll be able to determine if any of the plants are female. He'll discard the males and grow the females to flower to see what kind of buds they produce—how high the yield is and how potent the marijuana is.

That afternoon Aaron Morales, the grower from nearby Eureka, stops by to visit Jodrey. A local doctor told him about a strain called Cannatonic that is high in CBD. Cannatonic is a combination of other strains: MK Ultra, which lore has it originated with the US government and is a combination of Colombian, Mexican, and Southeast Asian strains, and G13 Haze, an indica. Morales ordered some Cannatonic seeds so he could grow them and test them out. He grew 20 plants and 11 of them showed some promise.

Downstairs Morales spreads 11 Ziploc bags containing the buds from each of those plants on the table to show Jodrey. The buds were tested for THC and CBD levels. Incredibly, each of the 11 bags contained almost totally different marijuana. The THC levels ranged from 0.3 percent to 26 percent and CBD levels ranged from 1 percent to 20 percent. Some buds smelled fruity and sweet, like pineapple; others, spicy like sandalwood. Still others were almost floral. One plant produced leafy buds that were spread out across the stem while most of the rest produced buds that were tight and full.

"I literally got 19 different plants," says Morales. "The only thing I can say is that they did not stabilize the strain."

Morales walks Jodrey through the buds he got from each of the 11 plants, discussing which ones might show some promise for bud production and for leaf growth for those who use leaves to make juice. Drinking the juice of cannabis leaves is a new approach gaining popularity here, but largely unheard of elsewhere, for those who are looking for the medicinal effects of CBD without the high of THC, which is not activated unless the plant is heated by burning or cooking. "You can tell which one I really liked by how little is left," Morales says with a laugh, wagging a nearly empty bag at Jodrey. "It's good, dude. It's really tasty. It reminds me of Salmon Creek, the smell, you know."

Jodrey picks up the bud and holds it up to his nose. "Oh, hell yeah! Old Salmon Creek, that's nice," he says, referring to a popular local strain named after a road populated with growers in Southern Humboldt County.

"I love that one. I mean, it grows a little wild," says Morales.

"That's alright, you can stake it," says Jodrey.

"Yeah, but look at the bud it produces," says Morales, turning the bud around in his fingers. "You know, it's not fluffy bud."

Jodrey picks out three of Morales' strains that he wants to grow at the dispensary—two that are high in THC with significant amounts of CBD and one that is high in CBD with little THC.

Morales doesn't earn anything by tinkering around with these strains. No one would buy the buds from these plants because he has such small amounts from each plant and, given the vast variation, he can't really say what strain they are so there is not yet much market for them. But he is using the most promising of these plants to experiment with breeding in order to refine and stabilize the strain—something that may pay off further down the line if he is able to develop a CBD-rich strain. He's investing his time and money because he thinks the potential for helping people with these high-CBD strains is important, as does Jodrey.

Morales gives the leaf from his plants—a byproduct that he does not sell anyway—to someone he knows with multiple sclerosis. "The guy that I deal with could not hold his urine," he tells Jodrey and me. "After six weeks of juicing, he doesn't have a problem. He can go to the bathroom when he wants to."

"That's a big difference in quality of life when you don't have to wear adult diapers" says Jodrey. "I've noticed with these patients, they are struggling so hard to survive and some of them come in here and they are fighting for their lives. I see them and it's like their hair is falling out of their head and I'm like, 'Bro, we are going to hook you up.' These guys are tough. They are not screwing around. They are motivated. They know they are going to go, they just want to go with some dignity. Through cannabis they are finding relief and in some cases subtle remission. It's just crazy to witness it firsthand."

"You almost don't believe it until you see it," says Morales.

It is this kind of firsthand experience that motivates many of the growers here. Regardless of the science—for example, there are few studies that examine how THCA, the non-psychoactive form of THC before it is heated, works in the body and none that examine the effects of cannabis juice on patients—many of these growers have seen the benefits of cannabis firsthand. They genuinely embrace the idea of helping people with this plant. And, of course, many of these growers have been able to find a second act for themselves, one with a very altruistic theme. People who began by growing and selling drugs, living their lives outside of the law, are now cast in a much more favorable light—as providers of important medicine, abiding by state law and pushing back against an intolerant federal government.

In the dispensary, Jodrey has thousands of cuttings from about 40 to 50 different strains on hand at any given time. The clone business is important to the dispensary's survival. The potted ones sell for $15 apiece, those just rooted in cubes sell for $10. The plants are relatively inexpensive to create and grow and they turn around quickly—about two weeks from cutting until they are ready to sell. It is very complicated to grow 40 or 50 different strains of marijuana in the dispensary's single flowering room since many of these strains take different amounts of time to flower completely—some as little as 50 days, others as long as 90 days. Jodrey cannot grow for everyone's needs or tastes. However, it is simple to have clones of 50 different strains available at any given time. It only requires a mother plant. If a patient has a particular need for a rare strain, Jodrey can sell him a clone to grow on his own. In many ways the mothers and clones are the heart of this business.

In a room upstairs, trays of tiny plants sit on metal shelves beneath long fluorescent tube lights. The trays are covered with arched plastic lids, like the ones you'd find on the bacon tray at an all-you-can-eat breakfast buffet. They trap the moisture in with the plants.

I sit down at a card table while Jodrey picks out a mother plant, one from a strain called Pot of Gold, an indica from Afghanistan crossed with Skunk #1 that he says is high yielding and relatively easy to grow. The first step to making clones is something Jodrey calls the snap test. Pinching a branch with his thumbnail against his finger, he breaks off a branch low down on the main stalk. The end of the shoot is almost woody and, he says, too fibrous to root quickly. At the top of the plant, the stalks are too new and not fibrous enough. Those about midway up are about right. The stalk breaks off cleanly without the woody fiber found in the more mature shoots and will root quickly. The goal, he says, is to take cuttings that are similar so they all root at about the same pace.

Then Jodrey shows me how to cut. It's important to avoid cutting the branch off at the main stem, he says. You always want to leave a node where the branch meets the stem, which will allow for a new stem to sprout quickly. Otherwise you are limiting the mother plant's ability to quickly produce new branches to cut and your own ability to make new clones. I cut about a six-inch-long branch off the plant.

Jodrey sticks his clones into little foam cubes called floral foam, and lines them up side by side in trays that are then stacked on the shelves. Each plant does not have a lot of room in which to grow leaves. And that is not the goal at this stage of development. He wants the plants to sprout roots. So, the leaves must be trimmed to fit into the tight accommodations in the tray. He shows me a simple technique. I place the plant in the palm of my hand, make a loose fist around it, and slide my hand up the stem until the leaves are pushed up into a bunch. I then lay a pair of scissors on the top of my forefinger at the top of my fist and clip off the protruding leaves so they are a uniform length and missing their readily identifiable spindly fingers. Then I snip the end of the shoot off at a 45-degree angle where it hits the bottom of my fist so it has a fresh cut before going into the foam. That way all of the clones I cut will be roughly the same height so none of them will out-compete the others for light in the tray. I poke the stem into the cube and place it in the tray and move on to the next one.

The clones go into a tray filled with perlite. The roots will grow down and out through the foam towards the perlite. Making sure that the clones are producing strong roots before they are sold is vital, says Jodrey. Removing the lids and aerating the plants and feeding them nutrients too early can lead to incomplete rooting and unhealthy clones. "If you sell those to people and they have catastrophic failure, that is your failure," says Jodrey. "What I've learned with cultivation is if the customer does well, it is their genius and if the customer does poorly, it is my fault."

Next I sit down at a long table across from Robert Wright. He's a 56-year-old retired truck driver, writer, and musician who has been volunteering at the dispensary for several months. He's got short, gray hair and a closely cropped gray beard. He takes a tray of clones off the shelf and we begin cleaning them up by pulling off dead leaves and separating them, readying them to be potted and sold.

When Wright retired, he decided that he wanted to get involved in the medical marijuana business so he came out to California. "What is going on out here is just fascinating," he tells me. "History is being made and this is the place to be." He drove up and down the state visiting different dispensaries but didn't find any as inviting as this one. Wright says that here he finally found a place that would teach him how to grow the plant and understand the business, a place where he could be part of a cannabis community. "Wow, it was great," he says. "They welcomed me with open arms."

Wright hands me a cube of floral foam with two clones poking out of it. In each of these cubes, one is inevitably a little taller and more robust than the other. We clip the cubes in half, pull off discolored leaves, and discard the few plants that have withered away and are unusable. Then the taller plants are grouped together for sale and the less robust ones are grouped together to be grown at the dispensary. Jodrey says that he always keeps the less robust ones for himself to make sure that the customers are happy.

Then Wright shows me how to pot the clones of Blueberry Headband. Next to the table is a large plastic trough filled with potting soil and small plastic pots. We fill each of the pots about halfway with soil, drop in the clone and the foam cube that it has rooted in and fill in the dirt around the clone. Then, gently, we tap each pot to get the dirt to settle. The dirt needs to be a few centimeters below the rim so the pots don't overflow when they are watered.

Wright and I settle in and begin to work. We're soon joined by another volunteer, a woman who has long blond hair and is wearing a tie dye t-shirt—the first tie dye I've seen in the dispensary. As we sit around the table, we sink into the rhythm of potting the plants, stopping only to make sure that each tray is properly labeled.

At the end of the day, Jodrey and I sit upstairs cutting clones. Talking with me is strange for him. Jodrey came of age in the underground, illegal industry. For decades he grew under the radar, outside of the law. In those years, smart growers kept their heads down, their mouths shut, and grew their pot. Those who talked too much often found themselves in handcuffs. But now that the industry is changing, now that growing marijuana here, in a dispensary or with a doctor's recommendation in relatively small amounts elsewhere, is no longer targeted by local law enforcement, growers are starting to speak up. They have to. With the industry moving towards legalization and towards the norms of business with accounting, record keeping, tax bills, with the need to comply with zoning laws and restrictions set up by local government, growers have to start speaking with each other and with the outside world. They need to come together to lobby local government, to organize with each other. But many of those who came of age in the illegal industry are terrified of even associating themselves with dispensaries operating in compliance with state law.

"I know people who won't even come into the dispensary," Jodrey tells me. "They are terrified of the place, terrified of the situation, terrified of coming out of the woodwork." When Jodrey talks to the media, as he does from time to time, it's even worse. "People step back and look at me in horror as if I was so hot they were going to get burned by my fumes," Jodrey says. But, he says, it has to be done. People need to see this as normal. Growers, those who run dispensaries, smokers, medical users, everyone involved in the business is just a normal person, he says.

Just as important to Jodrey is educating the next generation of growers. More and more people like contract grower Luke and retired truck driver Wright are coming here and entering the business. Humboldt and Mendocino counties are two of the few places where small-scale growers can operate with little fear of arrest. But many of these new growers have no idea what they are doing. Grow houses have burned to the ground thanks to bad wiring. Fuel to run diesel generators for large off-the-grid operations has leaked into streams. Waterways have been fouled with fertilizer. Poorly informed growers who are looking to get rich quick have done a lot of damage. And the market is so tight right now that only the best marijuana is getting bought in dispensaries and even on the black market. Plenty of people who see gold in the green buds of the cannabis plant are bound to end up broke. So, Jodrey wants to do what he can to help these people out by mentoring them here. While he is paid here, it is little, he tells me, compared to what he would make in the illegal market or as an independent medical grower. He is doing this work less for the money than because he feels it is important.

Luke, who began volunteering here in 2010, now earns a living thanks to what he learned at the dispensary. He tells me that he plans to bring in $100,000 in 2011 managing grows for other people. "Volunteering at HPRC has been incredibly valuable. If you just sit up there and cut clones, so many people come in over the course of a week with so many different questions. You get to watch people like Kevin and the other gardeners deal with those questions," Luke tells me. "Even though I've only been doing this for a year, I've seen more than people that have been doing this for 20 years."

Luke's experience here is just what Jodrey is hoping to achieve. His goal is to improve the knowledge base, and ultimately the quality of responsible growing here in Humboldt, one person at a time, with the hope that if growers here continue to improve they may be better able to weather the changes coming their way from the increasing sophistication of the medical market to the radical change that state legalization could bring. "I've always been a conduit for information," Jodrey tells me. "I take information in and I get it out to others so that they can benefit. This way my region does better. We all do better. This way, when I'm an old guy, I'll be able to look at the region and say, 'Hey, we survived.'"

11 THE FUTURE OF CANNABIS

It's never a good idea to make predictions about when California or another state will legalize marijuana. Jorge Cervantes told me that when he started writing his indoor grow guide in the early 1980s, he was convinced that marijuana would be legal nationally in five years. Many of those I spoke to expected it to be legal long ago. Yet, at the same time, the very same people express surprise at how close it has come to actually being legalized in California. That dissonance may be because the growers and breeders here live their lives in two totally separate worlds. Mostly they live in the world of cannabis where everyone they know smokes, where most people they socialize with grow marijuana, where some have grown up around the plant since they were babies. Marijuana is no stranger to them than Coca-Cola is to the rest of us. Marijuana is so present and available that it is completely unremarkable, like a bottle of Coke in the fridge. And, of course, whenever these growers and breeders leave their cannabis enclaves, they may be struck by how different mainstream society is. People, even lots of people, may smoke or have smoked at one time, but it is not something they do or even talk about openly. Cannabis is normal and abnormal, accepted and rejected all in the same breath. Despite this dichotomy, there is little question that after the close loss in the 2010 California election, legalization initiatives will continue to appear on ballots in cannabis-friendly states. With more states approving medical marijuana initiatives, the plant is reaching even more people in a normalized, regulated way. These laws allow cannabis entrepreneurs to get their sea legs in a smaller, though less certain market, than if they had to face an open market of tens of millions in a place like California. From a business perspective, medical marijuana laws are training wheels for potential future legalization. They provide businesses with some experience in how to navigate the uncertainties that come with specializing in a product that is outlawed by the federal government while it is allowed at the state and local level.

But what would legalization look like? The ballot initiatives in Colorado and Washington in 2012, and those sure to come in other states where majorities of residents support legalization, are likely to have a lot to say about possession, consumption, and even distribution of cannabis, but few are likely to say much about growing. That's because when voters say they support legalization, it usually means that they support legalizing one's ability to purchase small amounts of cannabis. There is also some agreement about how people should be able to purchase it—through cooperatives or dispensaries or some other regulated outlet rather than at a convenience or grocery store. But no one really wants to talk about growing.

Ethan Nadelmann, director at the Drug Policy Alliance, which advises on medical and legalization initiatives, is unsure how growers will play into all of this. When we meet in his organization's Manhattan office, he tells me that the Drug Policy Alliance's priority is creating laws that ensure that people will no longer be arrested for possession of small amounts of marijuana. "In terms of a hierarchy of values, the number one value is that no one should be punished for consuming marijuana responsibly," he says. "And second, you should be able to obtain marijuana in a legal way. Those are the two overriding things." But when it comes to growing your own—a plant or two in the backyard, for example—that is not the highest priority for his organization: "It's not at the same level of hierarchy," Nadelmann says.

Home cultivation can be a problem for voters and law enforcement. Indoor cultivation can cause electrical fires if it's not done properly. The environmental damage from indoor growing is an increasing concern given the incredible amounts of electricity indoor grows can consume. As much as 3 percent of California's electricity is used for indoor cannabis cultivation. And, marijuana growing, whether it's on a Mendocino mountaintop, in a backyard, or in a San Francisco loft, can attract thieves. People have been stealing marijuana as long as other people have been growing it. Many of the growers I met began cultivating marijuana in their teens. Some of them would like everyone to be able to grow their own plants—a kind of self-sufficient ideal that harkens back to the plant's back-to-the-land roots. But Kenny from Trichome Technologies maintains that there are just too many public safety problems. When someone grows in their backyard, he says, "some kid two doors down is going to steal it. And you are probably going to protect it and then someone can get hurt," he tells me. "You then become a public nuisance."

The question of commercial growing, who regulates it, or how it occurs, is rarely even discussed at the policy level and is often not well defined in the legislation. It's like legalizing drinking and regulating bars and liquor stores while refusing to mention how breweries and distilleries will be licensed and regulated. Even if marijuana becomes legal in California or another state, it may be quite some time before anyone has a clear understanding of how it can be legally cultivated, prepared, and distributed and what agencies might oversee production and create the standards by which the product is grown, processed, and made ready for sale like any other agricultural product.

Outdoor growers are concerned that the problems they have with the medical market will only be magnified should marijuana be legalized for broad use. California growers today benefit from a kind of protectionism created by the conflicting federal prohibition of the plant and the state's medical exceptions. On a federal level the plant is illegal. And certainly the majority of cannabis sold in this country is sold illegally. But small-scale growing, at least in the most cannabis-heavy areas of California, is tolerated. The legal gray zones keep the real investment dollars and large operators out of the market, keeping production relatively small scale. And that inherent risk keeps prices inflated. Even if prices have been falling recently, they are still remarkably high. At $1500 a pound, marijuana is still three times as expensive as truffles. Legalization could change that. The protection provided by the limited threat of arrest by local law enforcement would disappear (and it could disappear entirely, depending on how the federal government reacts). Though large, established companies would be unlikely to get into the market if cannabis were just legalized at the state level but remained illegal at the federal level, there would certainly be more investment dollars and larger-scale growing than was the case in 2011. Supply would increase and prices would plummet. And that shift would likely result in a major shake-up of the market. As Cervantes, who has been watching the industry for decades, told me, "The smart and the strong will survive and will be able to produce more efficiently."

The San Francisco grower, Marco, with his high-tech indoor growing system hidden inside his old warehouse, has tailored his business to meet the needs of the dispensary market here and, given his business background and interest in the kinds of technology that can help him increase both efficiency and output, he certainly stands a chance of faring well as the market here evolves. One afternoon, while I'm visiting Marco, his friend James drops by (he asks that I not use his last name). He's tan, wearing a loose-fitting tank top. His hair is pushed up with styling gel. He is friends with Marco but is only 24, wide-eyed, and earnest. He has a child-like enthusiasm about him and he looks more club kid than pot grower.

James has a long-standing interest (as long-standing as any interest can be for a 24-year-old) in alternative medicine and believes that cannabis is only one element, though an important one, in a more holistic approach to wellness and healing. Despite his young age, James is a bit of a serial entrepreneur. He runs a Web development company. He also consults with dispensaries on how to make diet, lifestyle, and alternative medicine part of their patient services. He divides his time between San Francisco, New York, and Spain. Recently he has taken a great interest in better understanding what strains of cannabis work best for which conditions. He has been surveying patients at a number of dispensaries to better understand their preferences. But even if patients find a compatible strain for their condition, they face another problem. After testing strains at some of the dispensaries, James discovered a remarkable variation in the cannabinoid profile within individual strains sold at different dispensaries—Blueberry or Headband at one dispensary is just not the same as it is at another dispensary due to different growing conditions, seed stock, or plants that are called by one name but are really another. So, he has begun collecting seeds of landrace strains, traveling to Mexico, South America, Europe, and California. His hope is to use these pure landrace strains to recreate popular strains like Sour Diesel or OG Kush to ensure that they are true to their genetic heritage. He hopes to create some consistency so patients know what they are getting. "We want to journey back to the root and start from there, making real Sour Diesel, real OG Kush, so it is what it is supposed to be from the start," he tells me.

While we talk, James takes out his iPad and shows me pictures of a fully automated greenhouse the size of a football field. Blinds on the side automatically rise and fall and a ceiling shade automatically retracts and extends when triggered by light sensors and timers. Sunlight can enter through the glass walls and ceiling. High-pressure sodium lights are switched on only when needed. The climate can be perfectly controlled just as it is in Marco's grow rooms beneath our feet. These large-scale greenhouses use all of the advantages of indoor technology with the added benefit of natural sunlight, which keeps costs down. Growers can harvest four crops in a year (six if they put plants through the vegetative stage in a separate facility) just as indoor growers can.

James has partnered with a Los Angeles dispensary to grow marijuana in Humboldt. And with the help of a lot of heavy equipment, he erected an immense greenhouse like the one he just showed me. In his high-tech, backwoods hideaway, and in indoor grow sites in San Francisco, he is growing organic marijuana for the patients in the Los Angeles dispensary. These large-scale greenhouses have a lot of benefits. Growers can control climate and keep buds protected from the weather like indoor growers can, but they work on a scale that allows them to cut costs and produce year-round. "The product looks better, tastes better, and smells better than outdoor," he says.

James hedges a bit on exactly how much is being grown here. He says that all of these sites have master growers and that they grow both outdoors in Humboldt as well as in the greenhouse. They grow large plants in the greenhouse to keep the numbers as low as they can but his sense is that the federal government is too focused on massive cartel grows to bother with medical grows under 999 plants. But the questionable legality of all of this bothers him. "My intention is not be Pablo Escobar," he says. "It is to help people heal. But I am scared that at any moment the DEA or someone will want to make an example of me. I do not want to go to jail." As a result he's considering relocating to Spain to help develop the medical cannabis seed industry there.

James wants to grow marijuana that patients can trust—cannabis that is the strain it purports to be, that is consistent, harvest to harvest, that is grown organically. That, he says, is the bare minimum required if he is to provide medicine to sick people in anything approaching a professional manner. This concern and approach may well mark the beginning of a significant shift in the way growers and breeders think about their jobs. And James, utterly unlike the old school outlaws and hippies of the north coast I've already met, may well represent an important new kind of grower—one with the funds and entrepreneurial focus required to succeed in many businesses.

Lots of growers are eyeing such large high-tech greenhouses as the future of the industry. It's one way to move from a decentralized, unregulated industry to one that adheres to more standards in a controlled environment, one that might be easer to regulate. That is not to say that marijuana grown outdoors cannot be both consistent and safe. After all, nearly all of our grains, fruits, and vegetables are produced outdoors and are regulated and overwhelmingly safe. But that is also not left up to chance. All food products, whether they are raw vegetables or processed foods or food products like juice or even beer are closely regulated and adhere to basic industry standards that govern how they are handled from the farm to the table.

In contrast, there is no such regulation for marijuana. It is produced, cured, and trimmed in people's homes with no set of standards, rules, or oversight beyond what the individual grower feels is appropriate. That marijuana is later sold in dispensaries throughout the state. What is occurring today with marijuana is, in many ways, the equivalent of having people who have made beer with a homebrew kit distribute it to supermarkets and liquor stores. Today buyers are relying on the honesty and good practices of thousands and thousands of growers. Many of those growers are good at what they do. Some are even great, but that does not mean that everyone is. No one monitors growing practices to determine what sort of chemicals growers can and can't add. No one requires them to list what chemicals or additives they use. There are no standards for production and, when faced with the potential loss of a crop from disease or pests or simply the possibility of boosting production and earning more money, any grower can be tempted to add chemicals when no one is looking. Many still do it as a matter of course.

Some dispensaries have tried to take control by testing the marijuana that comes in and examining it for mold or other damage. Some even keep track of the producer for each purchase so any problems can be traced back to the grower. Some prefer to buy marijuana that has received the Clean Green certification—the closest thing there is to an organic label for marijuana. Though the certification is designed to create a set of standards based on the practices of organic agriculture, the program is voluntary and remains small—at the beginning of 2012 there were only 49 growers participating. The industry has created some level of self-regulation and it is far better than the total chaos that reigns in a completely underground market of street-corner dealers. But for some that is not enough. Kenny, the co-owner of Trichome Technologies, thinks that cannabis growing needs to move beyond the small-scale, decentralized model that developed due to the underground market. "I don't want to put those people in Humboldt out of business," Kenny says. "I want huge cultivation facilities in the central valley, and I'll go hire all of them." Kenny has some experience with this through his partnership in Better, which grows marijuana for Israel's Ministry of Health in just this sort of massive greenhouse.

It is schemes such as these that tend to rub the growers in Humboldt and Mendocino the wrong way. It's unlikely many of these growers would want to give up their bucolic mountaintop retreats to move to Fresno to work for Kenny. They would likely take great offense at the very idea. Instead, many of them are looking for ways to find their own place in this changing economy.

In some ways outdoor growers have come full circle. In the early 1970s, before the war on drugs, the first generation of back-to-the-landers were able to just stick a marijuana plant in the garden in full sun without worrying. Now, 40 years later, they can once again cultivate in the full sun and now they can grow dozens of plants instead of just a few. Without much investment beyond a few hundred dollars for seeds or clones (if they don't produce their own) as well as not insignificant costs for irrigation systems, soil and organic nutrients, they can harvest pounds—as much as five pounds per plant or even more from some strains when they get full sun. It's efficient. It's relatively environmentally friendly and it supports whole communities in an otherwise economically depressed region. "There are a lot of regular people doing it that have been doing it for years," Sean tells me. By regular people, he means working people who harvest small crops year in and year out rather than risk-taking big-dollar growers. "The regular people are the ones who spend their money in the local markets and keep things here afloat. That's been the economic engine here for a long time," he says.

A legal market will likely create major challenges for growers like Sean. When I ask Richard Lee, the founder of Oaksterdam University who was behind the 2010 legalization initiative, about the future of those outdoor growers like Sean should a legalization initiative eventually pass here, he does not offer them much hope. "Outdoor is out. We know that it sucks," Lee says. "Customers don't like it. It's not as high quality. It's just not good."

Lee is echoing the popular sentiment about outdoor marijuana. Of course, a lot of indoor marijuana is not high quality either. Some think the differences are more a question of marketing than the quality of the actual product. Most outdoor marijuana is not as pristine looking as its indoor counterpart—it may suffer from the accumulation of rain, dust, and other organic elements that fall on it as it grows outside. But others say that if it is the right strain, grown and cured with care, it actually has the potential to be a much more desirable product than indoor. Outdoor marijuana can be far more powerful with a longer lasting high than indoor, possibly because the trichomes develop under natural sun. And if the crop is well tended and the right strains are grown in the right areas, they can look nearly as pristine as indoor marijuana.

Joey Burger, the founder of the Humboldt Growers Association, for one, welcomes the competition in an open marketplace. He says that Humboldt's outdoor growers produce a highly desirable product. "We grow high-quality, boutique outdoor bud that Humboldt is famous for," he says. "I want to compete. I want to take on Richard Lee." Part of the problem, says Kevin Jodrey from the Humboldt Patient Resource Center, is that outdoor growers are failing to adapt to the new market. They need to do a better job of keeping abreast of what strains are marketable. They need to tend to their crops, for example by putting hay or another mulch down to keep dust to a minimum. And, most important, they have to have a better understanding of what strains are going to perform the best in their growing environment. It is simple for an indoor grower to decide that OG Kush, for example, is hot and just grow that, but OG Kush may not work well in the conditions where an outdoor grower lives. So, they might be better off finding another slightly less popular strain that is better bred for where they live. Outdoor growers need to balance popularity with plant characteristics in a way that indoor growers do not. For example, Jodrey explains, if a grower is in a foggy coastal area, he could plant Royal Kush, which has a higher resistance to mold and powdery mildew than other strains. If growers are worried about early rains, they could plant a fast-maturing plant like Pineapple Train Wreck, which is usually ready to harvest in mid September. Those who have a ridge-top plot that gets full sun might plant OG Kush, Sour Diesel, or Headband, crops in high demand that require lots of sun and finish around November. Put those crops in shaded or foggy areas and they will not grow well and will not sell well. "If you grow the right strain in the right situation, you'll have a product that is superior to indoor," says Jodrey.

Steve DeAngelo, the founder of Harborside Health Center in Oakland, says that outdoor growers must excel at what they do because they are working against a common perception that they produce an inferior product, one that can look different from the buds that buyers are used to. It's not unlike the issue that organic farmers faced when their less than perfect-looking produce was compared to the immaculate, uniform crops produced by traditional agriculture. In that instance it took changes on both sides of the equation—organic produce has become better looking and consumers changed their ideas about what qualities mattered. The health benefits of organically grown produce became valued and consumers began to value flavor over appearance. It will likely take a similar shift on both the producer and consumer end of the equation for outdoor marijuana to become more competitive with that grown indoors.

When it comes to outdoor growers, DeAngelo says, they need to plant and harvest desirable strains and quality plants from those strains to ensure that the THC or CBD levels of the buds they sell are comparable or higher than those grown indoors. With more dispensaries starting to test and label the potency of their marijuana, outdoor growers have a chance to overcome some of the bias against appearance if they can consistently produce more potent marijuana than the competition. DeAngelo has already seen moderately priced outdoor strains do well. One batch he bought that was grown outdoors in Mendocino County had 16 percent THC and was priced the same as his lower THC indoor marijuana. It sold out in an hour.

DeAngelo also launched a campaign to help educate both

growers and consumers about the environmental impact of growing cannabis indoors, particularly the massive amount of energy that results from running lights, ventilation, and climate control systems. The San Francisco grower, Marco, for example, for all of his tech savvy, actually dumps hot water down the drain when he turns on his water heater to create carbon dioxide for his plants. The heating costs and carbon footprint are one thing, the fact that he wastes water in California where water is the single most fought-over resource would certainly rub some the wrong way (he does have plans to begin routing the warmed water into the building's traditional hot water heater). Environmentally conscious marijuana smokers are likely to be concerned about these issues and in turn may gravitate towards outdoor marijuana the way they gravitate towards fair trade products or organic produce, DeAngelo argues.

Marketing will be incredibly important. Marijuana produced outdoors has one unique attribute, says DeAngelo. The plant grows particularly large clusters of buds called colas. Because outdoor plants are much, much larger than those grown indoors they produce more flowers in larger clusters than indoor plants. As a result, their colas are much larger too. Usually trimmers break these down, snipping the buds off the stems and mixing them together into pounds. DeAngelo wants to contract with growers to buy the first five or six inches of the colas from their outdoor plants. He wants to put them in special glass jars engraved with a slogan like "Premium, Select, First-Cut, Sun-Grown Cannabis," and display them prominently in his dispensary. A presentation of top-quality marijuana like that will create the kind of allure of a special reserve single malt scotch, he says. By marketing the colas as something special, DeAngelo is working to find new attributes of this well-known plant to appeal to buyers. "We are going to change the idea that outdoor cannabis is something inferior. It's not really inferior," says DeAngelo. "The reason it got that reputation is because people have had to grow it in the shade. Some of the very best cannabis I have ever smoked in my life is outdoor cannabis that was grown in the full sun."

Marketing, it turns out, is something that a lot of growers are talking about these days. Even in the quasi-legal world of medical marijuana, marketing can help promote a brand, develop a desire for a particular strain, or even build loyalty to a particular grower. Estes has hired a graphic designer to create a logo for his strain. His logo reads, "The Original Grand Daddy Purp Since 2003" to differentiate his strain from other Grand Daddy Purps sold by competitors. "I have a brand and I am trying to make sure that people recognize it, that they know it is the Grand Daddy Purp, my strain, the original, not someone else's," Estes says. "We go to hemp and medical marijuana events, we show people the bud and talk about growing." Other growers do similar things. Lawrence Ringo puts pictures of himself dwarfed by his massive cannabis plants on his webpage for the Southern Humboldt Seed Collective and, like Estes, does the conference circuit.

Some growers are turning to social media. Since online marijuana forums are so popular, growers are using them to promote their products. Nomaad, the Lake County grower, posts photos of his plants and buds online to try to drum up interest in the strains that he is selling. So does Burger. He spends a lot of time posting photos of his and his friends' immense outdoor plants to online message boards. The readers on these boards, he says, "are worshipping these guys growing in their closets. I started to show some pictures of what is going on up here and it blows people's minds. Nobody has ever pulled back the redwood curtain and shown them what's up here in Humboldt." Burger says that some of his images have gotten over 200,000 views. He promotes his own strains and he does not sell seeds or clones of these plants so he is the only source for this particular strain of marijuana—usually variants on Kush and Sour Diesel. He says people walk into dispensaries asking for those varieties. "I'm building up a name brand," he says. And that online presence helped open the door to at least one dispensary that he now sells to regularly. "You have to be on those forums. You have to hype up that stuff. You have to go to trade shows," says Burger. "You have to make the effort."

Burger says that Humboldt and Mendocino could become a sort of Napa Valley for cannabis—boutique tasting rooms, farm tours, even zip lines above the fields. And he expects his high-quality outdoor marijuana to cater to much the same market that Napa Valley caters to today. "We want the baby boomer who smoked Humboldt weed in the 1970s and 1980s. Now he's retired, got some arthritis. He spends all of his paycheck at Whole Foods buying organic food and a nice bottle of wine," says Burger. "That is the market we want."

Certainly legalization in the state could bring an incredible economic bounty. Dale Gieringer, state director of California NORML, says that the wine industry might be a comparable industry to compare the potential impact of legalizing marijuana in the state. According to the Wine Institute, California's wine industry had $12.3 billion in retail sales in 2008 and that generated $51.8 billion in economic activity, including 309,000 jobs, $10.1 billion in wages, and $2 billion in tourist expenditures. Gieringer says a regulated marijuana industry that is smaller, about 30 percent of the size of the wine industry (based on the number of regular marijuana smokers estimated by the government to be in California), could result in $12 billion to $18 billion in economic activity, 60,000 to 100,000 jobs, and $2.5 to $3.5 billion in legal wages.

Of course that vision of the future and other optimistic commercial scenarios all assume that things proceed along the same trajectory they are on now—an increasing acceptance of marijuana use and changes in the law that permit an ever more open culture of cultivation and consumption. But there is another model, one that could cause things to change in a very different way. GW Pharmaceuticals is already nearing US approval for its Sativex product that provides relief for muscle contraction and tightness in MS patients. It is conducting research on a dozen different cannabinoids that may help address other health problems. The company has shown that it can bring in funding—its founder, Dr. Guy, says it has spent over $300 million on research alone. The company has proven that it can work well with regulators who are skeptical of cannabis and skeptical of its plant extract approach. It has a breeding program and seed bank unlike any other. Plenty of those in the cannabis world are wary of how its presence in the United States may change things.

The Drug Policy Alliance's Nadelmann says that early on, he felt that GW was open to the goals of the marijuana reform movement and the movement was happy about GW and the work it was doing. Finally, here was a company that was going to conduct solid scientific research on the medical benefits of the plant itself rather focusing on a single cannabinoid such as THC. "The fact that they are doing the research, identifying and proving marijuana's medical benefits and legitimizing marijuana as a medical product, that is all to the good," says Nadelmann. However, in subsequent years, he has changed his mind. "I think they decided there was a more oppositional relationship," he says of GW. There is always the concern that once Sativex is approved in the United States and other such extracts receive approval for various conditions, the logic behind medical marijuana laws will no longer be as compelling. Today the only way that those suffering from, say, cancer pain, can get cannabis is through some sort of medical marijuana dispensary system. If they live in a state that does not have a medical exemption, they must break the law to buy on the street. As many people have testified in legislative hearings on medical marijuana law, it is not unusual for parents to risk arrest to buy for their children, for children to buy for their elderly parents, for senior citizens to overcome great fear to even try smoking marijuana. No one wants to criminalize people looking for relief from pain or nausea. If Sativex and future cannabis extracts are approved by the FDA, there is little argument left in favor of creating an exemption for medical users. Those suffering from various conditions can just get a prescription from their physician for a cannabis extract and have it filled at the pharmacy. Nadelmann says that he is concerned that GW is in competition with the current medical marijuana dispensary system. Yet, he admits that GW, at least today, presents a mixed picture for medical marijuana advocates. "It is presumably good for people using marijuana for medical purposes since it provides standardization and research," he says. "How it relates to the larger movement—there has been fierce debate."

GW draws a bright line between its product and medical marijuana. Dr. Guy says the company is neutral when it comes to the debate over medical marijuana in this country. Nonetheless, he says his company has only helped to inform the debate over the medical use of cannabis. "We have elevated the quality of the science," he says. "The presence of precise and objective data about the medical benefits of the plant exists because of us—no one else is doing this." However, he is quick to point out that GW's research does not apply to smoked cannabis or food products laced with THC but instead to a "precise pharmaceutical approved by international regulatory authorities for its impact on a set of specific conditions." Dr. Guy says that the people who use Sativex are a distinct market—people who suffer from a particular set of symptoms, who want an FDA-approved drug (assuming it is approved in this country) prescribed to them by their physician. "Most patients with complex, chronic, and very serious conditions prefer all of their medications to be prescribed by a doctor, to understand what medication they are taking and what the side effects are," Dr. Guy says. These people, he says, will not show up at dispensaries looking for an alternative product.

Sativex, however, is a different kind of pharmaceutical. It is a plant extract, produced according to the company's precise guidelines. Its manufacturing environment is up to international pharmaceutical standards. The product is consistent, tested, and approved by regulators for use in half a dozen countries. But in the simplest sense, what the company is doing is grinding up the leaves and buds of cannabis plants from two strains, one high in THC and another high in CBD, extracting the cannabinoids, refining the extracts, and mixing the two together. The extraction process itself is nothing magical.

And because the product is an extract, DeAngelo says it will be in direct competition with the medical marijuana market. DeAngelo says that some people will choose synthetic THC, or Marinol. Much of the rest of the market will be taken up by what he calls nutraceuticals—extracts and concentrates that are not approved by the FDA but fit into the much looser and less regulated category of dietary supplements. A cannabis extract at your local dispensary compared to Sativex may be a bit like vale-rian root compared to Valium. Products like valerian root do not need to meet the same rigorous testing required by the FDA nor do they require a doctor's prescription. And some people, when they want to relieve anxiety, have a valerian root pill or valerian root tea instead of getting a prescription for Valium. (Despite the similarity in their names, Valium was not derived from vale-rian root. But the two do have similar effects on anxiety; vale-rian root's effect is more subtle.) DeAngelo imagines that people will be able to buy extracts at their local medical dispensary for much less than they would pay for Sativex. In 2011, patients at Harborside could buy a cannabis extract that is administered in a spray just like Sativex or by a dropper. It costs just $18 for about 10 doses. In the United Kingdom, the National Health Service spends the equivalent of $17 a day for an average patient's daily dose of Sativex—nearly the same price as an entire spray bottle at Harborside for a single day's worth of the drug. It is unclear how Sativex will be priced here. If it is approved, private insur-ance would pay for some of the cost, unlike cannabis, which is not covered by insurance policies. "The vast bulk of cannabis users are not going to need pharmaceutical grade production and would prefer nutraceutical quality," DeAngelo says. "I don't think Sativex is going to be able to compete with the nutraceuti-cal side of the market."

GW's potential business in the United States is predicated on marijuana prohibition, DeAngelo argues. Across the ocean, Dr. Guy doesn't think much about the US medical market, though he says that he is asked about it all the time. His competitors, he says, are pharmaceutical companies that make competing drugs for the symptoms that Sativex targets. The fact that he does it with cannabis is, in some ways, a coincidence. The plant has a long-standing medical history and has been remarkably poorly researched over the last few decades. Given that, Dr. Guy believes that cannabis is a very smart place to be putting a company's resources. The fact that he finds himself tangled up with those advocating change of medical marijuana laws can be baffling to him. "We are not going to wreck this market," he says. "We are addressing a part of the market that is outside or separate from the area that medical marijuana advocates are in," he says. But because GW is basing its business on this most controversial of plants, it is inevitable that it will be dragged into the debate. And, whether he likes it or not, Dr. Guy and his company will likely have a tremendous impact on the outcome of those debates and through its research and breeding, on the future of the plant itself.

GW is not the only company applying modern scientific research and techniques to cannabis. Others are also starting to drag the plant into the modern era. In fact, one company has already sequenced the cannabis genome. Kevin McKernan, the founder of Medicinal Genomics who directed research and development for the Human Genome Project, became interested in the plant because of the medical research coming out of GW Pharmaceuticals. Cannabis, he points out, is remarkably safe compared to other drugs, particularly pain medications. Many pain medications have a narrow therapeutic index—phenobarbital, which prevents seizures and relieves anxiety, has an index of 10. If something has a therapeutic index of 10, that means that 10 times the effective dose will kill 50 percent of animals in studies or cause toxicity in 50 percent of the humans studied. Cannabis is among the safest drugs with a therapeutic index of 1000.

"With many drugs you are threading the needle between helping the patients and killing them," he says. Cannabis is almost impossible to overdose on. McKernan, who also founded a company that provides low-cost gene sequencing, wanted to sequence the plant. His company has a lab in the Netherlands so it can work on the plant legally there. He approached a seed company called DNA Genetics about finding a pure indica plant to sequence. They gave him a strain called LA Confidential.

Medicinal Genomics is still trying to assemble and make sense of much of the genetic data it has on the plant. But as the work goes forward, McKernan says it has the potential to change the way that cannabis research and even breeding are conducted. Scientists can now know much more about the various cannabinoids from their genetic makeup. With the genome sequenced, some research can be done without direct access to the plant, just by using the gene sequence. And breeders can use this information to jumpstart their efforts. If a breeder wants to create strains high in particular cannabinoids, terpenes, or other qualities, they can screen entire crops of the plant for the ones with the desirable genetic traits. They no longer have to grow plants to full maturity to understand what traits they will express. This approach uses the knowledge contained in the DNA to guide traditional breeding approaches, says McKernan. It can speed up the process of creating new strains dramatically.

McKernan's ongoing research also has the potential to open the door to genetic engineering of cannabis plants. Breeders could skip traditional breeding and simply pick and choose the qualities they would like in the plant by inserting different genetic sequences. But that, of course would be incredibly controversial. According to Dr. Guy, GW has no plans to engage in genetic engineering of cannabis plants. For starters, genetic engineering in Europe has an incredibly bad name. And, he says that to take a cannabinoid that may appear in a 10th of a percent in a natural plant and simply engineer one where it is at 50 percent is pushing the plant too far. It's likely that a strain like that could never exist in nature and he can't safely begin testing extracts from such a plant. He would need to conduct new safety tests. Breeding a plant through a natural process to go from a 10th of a percent to 0.5 or 10 percent of a particular cannabinoid might take four or five years but would yield a plant that is much safer and easier to test and run trials with than an engineered one.

Genetic engineering or even using the genetic information to guide traditional breeding approaches, however, may give others the leg up they need to compete with GW. Given the dearth of cannabis seed banks available outside of the underground market, most legitimate businesses would have a hard time amassing the genetic stock necessary for a breeding program like GW's. That is part of what gives the company its edge over others. To find the seeds of these plants and breed them the old fashioned way would require a lot more than money; it would require deep connections into the cannabis underground. In contrast, anyone who can amass the necessary funding can start using the plant's genetic information to guide a breeding program or perhaps even genetically engineer cannabis strains high in any number of cannabinoids or with a particular terpene profile. So, with the genome sequenced, the possibility of genetically engineered cannabis strains is not necessarily around the corner, but it is a step closer to reality.

There are also those in the old cannabis underground who see new possibilities in merging existing technology with their knowledge gained over decades in the industry. Chimera, the Canadian breeder, sees a significant potential market for a technology that was developed for legal agriculture but was never adapted in any significant way. While the seed market is popular, most growers prefer to start from clones if they can. A clone will be an exact genetic copy of the mother plant and so growers avoid the variation that can be present in seeds, particularly those that are not well stabilized. Unfortunately it also means that any pathogens like molds or fungi in the mother plant can be passed along. The reach of clones is limited. They can't be mailed over long distances. The market for clones is really only a car ride's distance from the point of sale, which localizes the market.

Chimera has a better idea. He is working with Tom, who has been growing on Spyrock Road since the mid 1980s, to produce synthetic cannabis seeds. Synthetic seeds were first developed in the 1970s but are expensive to produce so never gained traction in the world of legal agriculture. But, given the value of cannabis, cost is less of an issue. And this technology could solve one of the biggest problems with large-scale cannabis production: it can enable growers to cultivate the exact same plant every time on a massive scale, something that will be important should the plant ever be legalized or put into widespread production for medical use. "If you are growing 100 or 200 acres of marijuana, you want it to all be as identical as possible," says Chimera. "With cannabis, if you grow 100 acres, you are going to have an incredible degree of variation." A synthetic seed is essentially a clone in seed form so it enables a grower to produce the same product every time no matter how many they plant. In addition, synthetic seeds are created in vitro in a sterile environment so growers can be certain that they will not introduce pests or pathogens into their production sites.

These synthetic seeds are created by slicing off a piece of the earliest sprout of a new shoot from a plant grown in vitro and placing it in a jelly-like medium called agar. Seeds made this way can only be stored for up to about six months. They are "germinated" by adding a nutrient formula to the medium that includes sucrose, which is the byproduct of photosynthesis—what the plant lives on. With the sucrose in the medium, the plant can grow with little light, much as a seed does when it germinates. The seeds need to be started in a completely sterile environment.

By using this technology, exact genetic copies of particular plants could theoretically be shipped anywhere (though Chimera works legally in Canada and does not plan to ship internationally). "This is a way for delivering clones in seed form," says Chimera. "When I heard about this, it hit me like a lightning bolt that this is the way to go." Chimera is in the midst of putting together their lab and plans to begin production soon. If the technology is successful, Chimera and Tom could enable growers to obtain exact genetic replicas of the strains they want without wading through the variation that comes along with natural seeds. And, it creates the possibility for large-scale consistent production. Chimera is also working on new approaches to making synthetic seeds that would allow them to be stored for much longer, potentially allowing this to become a way to capture and preserve important genetic lines of the plant for use in the future, creating a living library of cannabis, something Tom has worked so hard to do for so long.

"Hopefully this technology will kick all of those people who don't know what they are doing out of the business," says Chimera. "All of this ad-hoc breeding and delivery of unstabilized hybrid strains has taxed the genetic resources of the plant. They are chipping away at our most valuable resource, the genome, and taking it apart with a chisel and fragmenting it into little pieces," says Chimera. Just as Tom dedicates his time to preserving old strains and maintaining the genetic integrity of the plant,

Chimera hopes their joint effort will serve a similar end. "Cannabis shouldn't just be another resource to be exploited," he says.

Tom is very excited about the possibilities of this partnership with Chimera. But, closer to his heart is the day-to-day rhythm of working with the plant. As he likes to say, at the end of the day he is a farmer. At his Spyrock Road ranch, he takes me for a walk around his cannabis garden. The front yard of his house, the area alongside his driveway is covered with plants. One group sits up against Tom's barn wall waiting to get transplanted into massive pots. He walks me inside the barn and it turns out to be as much an illusion as any movie set. Despite its two-story wall of peeling red paint on the outside, it has no roof. Inside, immense 300-gallon pots hold young marijuana plants. In the early morning mist, they are struggling upwards towards the light, most still a springtime pale green, still young with the full summer before them.

As we walk back towards another garden, I ask him about the possibility of legalization, the possibility that he and the other growers who have made their livelihood up here on this ridge with this plant may be chased out of the business. Tom, it turns out, is for it. "Anything that helps to mainstream cannabis, I'm all for it. I don't care if it puts me out of work. I'm creative enough to work around it," he tells me looking out across the valley. "I'm a fucking outlaw. I'm going to grow grass and be compensated for those efforts regardless of how any of this shakes out. I might have to get out the old travel book and throw darts at it to decide where to go, but believe me there are plenty of cannabis-deprived places that could use someone like me."

Unlike many who worry about how the loss of the plant could change this place, Tom is happy to choose the plant over the community if it comes to that. Despite his history here and his feeling for the community in which he has thrived for a quarter century, for Tom, the plant wins over the place without much of a second thought. And he plans to champion it through whatever future may come, hoping that eventually others can pick up where he has left off, taking his work and using it to better the plant for future generations. "I'm not scared of giving all of my lines away to people and making it public domain—even the playing field. Let's educate everybody. We're all on the same team," Tom says with a smile. "Let's move forward together."

BIBLIOGRAPHY

American Society of Addiction Medicine. 2010. The role of the physician in "medical" marijuana. Available at asam.org/pdf/Advocacy/MedMarijuanaWhitePaper20110314.pdf.

Anslinger, Harry J., and Will Oursler. 1961. *The Murderers: The Shocking Story of the Narcotics Racket, Its Rulers and Victims.* New York, NY: Avon Book Division.

Anslinger, Harry J., with J. Dennis Gregory. 1964. *The Protectors: Our Battle Against the Crime-Gangs.* New York, NY: Farrar, Straus.

Armentano, Paul (National Organization for the Reform of Marijuana Laws). 2005. Marinol vs. Natural Plant. Available at norml.org/component/zoo/category/marinol-vs-natural-cannabis.

Associated Press. 1988. U.S. to resume using paraquat on marijuana. Available at www.nytimes.com/1988/07/14/us/us-to-resume-using-paraquat-on-marijuana.html.

Booth, Martin. 2005. *Cannabis: A History.* New York, NY: Picador.

Brown, David Jay. 2011. DEA going to federal court for blocking medical marijuana research. *SantaCruzPatch* (7 October). Available at santacruz.patch.com/articles/dea-going-to-federal-court-for-blocking-medical-marijuana-research.

Bryant, Tim. 1993. DEA targets indoor pot growers. *St. Louis Post-Dispatch* (9 May): 1D.

California NORML. 2011. Cal. NORML estimates 750,000–1,125,000 medical marijuana patients in California. Available at canorml.org/news/cbcsurvey2011.html.

Central Valley California High Intensity Drug Trafficking Area Program. 2010. Marijuana production in California.

Cervantes, Jorge. 2006. *Marijuana Horticulture: The Indoor/ Outdoor Medical Grower's Bible.* Vancouver, WA: Van Patten Publishing.

Cervantes, Jorge. 2002. *Indoor Marijuana Horticulture: The Indoor Bible.* Vancouver, WA: Van Patten Publishing.

Cervantes, Jorge. 1984. *Indoor Marijuana Horticulture.* Portland, OR: Interport, U.S.A.

Clarke, Robert Connell. 1993. *Marijuana Botany: Propagation and Breeding of Distinctive Cannabis.* Oakland, CA: Ronin Publishing.

Controlled Substances Act, Pub. L. No. 91-513, Tit. II, 84 Stat. 1242 (21 U.S.C. 801 et seq.).

Council on Science and Public Health Report 3. 2009. Use of cannabis for medicinal purposes. American Medical Association, 2009 Interim Meeting.

Frank, Mel, and Rosenthal, Ed. 1978. *Marijuana Grower's Guide.* Berkeley, CA: And/Or Press.

Gallup. 2011. Record-high 50% of Americans favor legalizing marijuana use. Available at www.gallup.com/poll/150149/record-high-americans-favor-legalizing-marijuana.aspx.

Gallup. 2011. Doctor-assisted suicide is moral issue dividing Americans most. Available at www.gallup.com/poll/147842/doctor-assisted-suicide-moral-issue-dividing-americans.aspx.

Gettman, Jon. 2006. Marijuana production in the United States (2006). *Bulletin of Cannabis Reform* (December). Available at drugscience.org/bcr/archives.html.

Gieringer, Dale (California NORML). 2009. Marijuana legalization could yield California taxpayers over $1.2 billion per year. Available at www.canorml.org/background/CA_legalization2.html.

Hamm, Ernest D. 1973. *The Criminalization of Marihuana.* Undergraduate Thesis, Augusta College.

Hazekamp, Arno, and Franjo Grotenhermen. 2010. Review on clinical studies with cannabis and cannabinoids 2005–2009. *Cannabinoids* 5: 1–21.

Hoeffel, John. 2009. Los Angeles County D.A. prepares to crack down on pot outlets. *Los Angeles Times* (9 October). Available at articles.latimes.com/2009/oct/09/local/me-medical-marijuana9.

Holland, Julie, M.D., ed. 2010. *The Pot Book: A Complete Guide to Cannabis: Its Role in Medicine, Politics, Science and Culture.* Rochester, VT: Park Street Press.

Iversen, Leslie L. 2008. *The Science of Marijuana.* 2nd ed. New York, NY: Oxford University Press.

Johnston, Lloyd D., Patrick M. O'Malley, Jerald G. Bachman, and John E. Schulenberg. 2011. Demographic subgroup trends for various licit and illicit drugs, 1975–2010 (Monitoring the Future Occasional Paper No. 74). Ann Arbor, MI: Institute for Social Research. Available at monitoringthefuture.org/.

Kilmer, Beau, Jonathan P. Caulkins, Rosalie Liccardo Pacula, Robert J. MacCoun, and Peter H. Reuter. 2010. Altered state? Assessing how marijuana legalization in California could influence marijuana consumption and public budgets (Occasional Paper). Santa Monica, CA: RAND Drug Policy Research Center. Available at www.rand.org/pubs/occasional_papers/2010/RAND_OP315.pdf.

King, Jason. 2001. *The Cannabible.* Berkeley, CA: Ten Speed Press.

Laurel, Alicia Bay. 1970. *Living on the Earth.* Berkeley, CA: The Bookworks.

McPartland, John N., and Geoffrey W. Guy. 2004. The evolution of *Cannabis* and coevolution with the cannabinoid receptor—a hypothesis. In *The Medicinal Uses of Cannabis and Cannabinoids.* Eds. Geoffrey W. Guy, Brian A. Whittle, and Philip J. Robson. London, United Kingdom, and Chicago, IL: Pharmaceutical Press. 71–101.

McPartland, John M., and Patty Pruitt. 2002. Sourcing the code: searching for the evolutionary origins of cannabinoid receptors, vanilloid receptors, and anandamide. *Journal of Cannabis Therapeutics* 2 (1): 73–103.

Mehmedic, Zlatko, Suman Chandra, Desmond Slade, Heather Denham, Susan Foster, Amit S. Patel, Samir A. Ross, Ikhlas A. Khan, and Mahmoud A. ElSohly. 2010. Potency trends of 9-THC and other cannabinoids in confiscated *Cannabis* preparations from 1993–2008. *Journal of Forensic Science* 55: 1209–1217.

Merlin, Mark David. 1972. *Man and Marijuana*. Cranbury, NJ: A.S. Barnes.

Miller, Timothy. 1999. *The 60s Communes: Hippies and Beyond.* Syracuse, NY: Syracuse University Press.

Mills, Evan. 2011. *Energy Up in Smoke: The Carbon Footprint of Indoor Cannabis Production.* Available at evan-mills.com/energy-associates/Indoor_files/Indoor-cannabis-energy-use.pdf.

Montgomery, Michael. 2011. Feds to target newspapers, radio for marijuana ads. *California Watch* (12 October). Available at californiawatch.org/dailyreport/feds-target-newspapers-radio-marijuana-ads-13049.

National Organization for the Reform of Marijuana Laws. Medical marijuana. Available at norml.org/legal/medical-marijuana-2.

Renner, Susanne S., and Robert E. Ricklefs. 1995. Dioecy and its correlates in the flowering plants. *American Journal of Botany* 82 (5): 596–606.

Romero, Dennis. 2011. Marijuana dispensary numbers remain near 2009 high: Starbucks or weed, you'll find plenty of choices in Los Angeles. *LA Weekly Informer Blog* (2 December). Available at blogs.laweekly.com/informer/2011/12/marijuana_dispensaries_angeles_500_pot_shops.php/.

Russo, Ethan B. 2011. Taming THC: potential cannabis synergy and phytocannabinoid-terpenoid entourage effects. *British Journal of Pharmacology* 163: 1344–1364.

Siebert, Charles. 2011. Food ark. *National Geographic* (July): 108–131.

Sims, Hank. 2010. General Lee: Can Oaksterdam weed magnate Richard Lee push legalization over the top? *North Coast Journal* (29 July). Available at northcoastjournal.com/news/2010/07/29/general-lee/.

Sokolov, Raymond A. 1978. Nonfiction in brief, review of *Marijuana Grower's Guide* by Ed Rosenthal and Ed [*sic*] Frank. *New York Times* (16 April).

Substance Abuse and Mental Health Services Administration. 2011. Results from the 2010 National Survey on Drug Use and Health: Summary of National Findings. NSDUH Series H-41, HHS Publication No. (SMA) 11-4658. Rockville, MD: Substance Abuse and Mental Health Services Administration. Available at oas.samhsa. gov/NSDUH/2k10NSDUH/2k10Results.htm.

Time Magazine. 1978. Nation: Panic over paraquat. *Time Magazine* (May 1). Available at time.com/time/magazine/article/0,9171, 919548-1,00.html.

US Drug Enforcement Administration. 2010 Domestic Cannabis Eradication/Suppression Program Statistical Report. Available at www.justice.gov/dea/programs/marijuana_seizure_results.pdf.

US Drug Enforcement Administration. DEA Drug Seizures. Available at www.justice.gov/dea/statistics.html.

Verhoeckx, Kitty C. M., Henrie A. A. J. Korthout, A. P. van Meeteren-Kreikamp, Karl A. Ehlert, Mei Wang, Jan van der Greef, Richard J. T. Rodenburg, and Renger F. Witkamp. 2006. Unheated Cannabis sativa extracts and its major compound THC-acid have potential immuno-modulating properties not mediated by CB1 and CB2 receptor coupled pathways. *International Immunopharmacology.* 6: 656–665.

INDEX